SOUTH OF THE FORK

Fresh, simple-to-prepare recipes from The Junior League of Dallas

SOUTH OF THE FORK

The Junior League of Dallas, Inc.

Dallas, Texas

1987

The Junior League of Dallas is an organization of women committed to promoting voluntarism and to improving the community through the effective action and leadership of trained volunteers.

All proceeds from the sale of SOUTH OF THE FORK will be used to benefit community projects sponsored by the Junior League of Dallas, Inc.

To order additional copies of SOUTH OF THE FORK write to:

SOUTH OF THE FORK
The Junior League of Dallas, Inc.
8003 Inwood Road
Dallas, Texas 75209 3335

Design by Linda Eissler, Eisenberg, Inc., Dallas
Assisted by Randall Hill

Text by Ana Kehoe

Food and still life photography by Jim Olvera, Dallas
Assisted by Nancy Lockett
Additional photography by Sally Larroca

Library of Congress catalog card number: 86-62946

ISBN 0-9617677-0-7

First Printing: 40,000 copies June 1987

Printed in the United States of America by Heritage Press, Inc., Dallas

THE COOKBOOK COMMITTEE

ACKNOWLEDGMENTS

We wish to thank the following for their contributions of enthusiasm, energy, talent and generousity, without which this book would not have been possible.

Absolutely Necessary
Armstrong Elementary School
Mr. Rick Barry
Ben Morris Company
Mr. Darren Blanton
A Budding Success Florist
Bullard's Flowers
Dallas Country Club
Doak Walker Sports Center
Linda Eissler
French-Brown Floors
Gumps
Highland Park Antiques
Huey and Phillips Restaurant
   Supply
The Ivy House
Larsen Vardeman, Inc.

Marie Leavell
Mary McNab
Dr. Don Mauldin
Mr. Brian Medlock
Neiman-Marcus
Park Cities People
Plate and Platter, Inc.
Pollock Paper Company
Potted Palm
Register Antiques
Russell O'Neil
Stanley Korshak
Uncommon Market
Village Bakery
Coach "Whitey" Whitelock
Williams-Sonoma
Mr. George Works
Mr. Angus Wynne

COOKBOOK COMMITTEE

President
Peggy Carr

President Elect
Sally McPherson

Chairman
Sissy Alsabrook

Secretary
Debbie Begert

Treasurer
Jane Douglas

Publishing Coordinator
Sam Mauldin

Design Editor
Joan Smith

Testing Editors
Sherry Hortenstine
Betsy Cullum

Index Editors
Becky Good
Sissy Russell
Chris Redden

Print Editor
Ana Kehoe

Proofing Editors
Jann Scott
Peggy Barry
Di Ann Bartholow
Sharon Enderby

Computer Input Staff
Charlotte Hicks
Luann Sewell

Marketing Coordinator
Cherre Felton

P.R./Advertising Chairman
Logan Geeslin

Printed Materials Assistant
Kari Wade

Conventions Assistant
Kathryn Carter

Promotional Assistant
Mary Tabor

Accounts Chairman
Linda Wells

Accounts Assistants
Debbie Snell
Helen Puckett
Margo Exline

Special Events Chairman
Susan Campbell

Special Events Assistants
Paige Baten
Ann Carruth
Jaye Molsen
Peggy Pollock
Carol Utkov
Mary Williams

Members-at-Large
Kay Barry
Nancy Enlow
Charlotte Ball
Melinda Wynn
Amy Malin
Jane Fitch

Sustaining Advisors
Nancy Lemmon
Anne Greer
Carol Touchstone
Linda McElroy
Sally Wood

Cookbook Research Committee
Mary Ann Denton
Jenny Zimmerly
Leslie Conant
Becky Good

TABLE OF CONTENTS

TABLE OF CONTENTS

TABLE OF CONTENTS

INTRODUCTION

Generations ago Dallas territory was landmarked as "The Three Forks". Supposedly the nickname had nothing to do with the local chow, but it must have been a great watering hole. It was here the Trinity River branched into three streams and, according to jukebox legend, the pioneers who stuck around these parts were thirsty for adventure and hungry for success.

Today, pioneers still linger. While those of long ago have already staked their claims along the Trinity and left behind their blessings, there's a new generation of doers, can-doers, undaunted by risk. We sport bandanas or black ties, blue jeans in boardrooms; we're as much cowboy as corporate executive, and some of us even brag with a yankee accent. Our breed may savor traditions but we're not a traditional bunch. We take chances; go for broke.

In recent years Dallas has fascinated the world, and citizens from cities everywhere have introduced and intrigued us with the finest and freshest of international cuisines. Since the best way to any cowboy's heart is through his stomach, Dallas has adapted well to this new culinary frontier. Although you may recognize some recipes as favorites, we're not trying to refry old beans. We have included a few homespun classics because, after all, this is a city proud of her past. But, on the whole, SOUTH OF THE FORK applauds a more sophisticated cuisine.

Although Dallas palettes have grown more discerning over the decade, we still clap our hands, tap our toes and smack our lips at the thought of home cookin'. Dallas remains a pioneer to the bone. So, as they say SOUTH OF THE FORK . . . Bon(e) Appetit!

HOSPITALITY

HOSPITALITY

When it comes to hospitality, mum may be the flower but not the word. Spread smiles of welcome and new beginnings. A potpourri of sight and smell, tone and texture can be bundled into a basket to celebrate a housewarming. Along with dinner, tuck in some hospitality from the hardware store, like hammer, nails and oh yes, band-aids.

Once upon a time the rules of hospitality were as rigid and formal as crystal and white linen. But as the desire to please rather than impress one's guests evolved, hospitality grew as comfortable and casual as sharing bread, Brie and Burgundy on the back porch.

But, for many of us, even a lazy evening at home with friends is a luxury; we're either on the go, on the job or stuck in traffic. That's why we decided these menus should travel well. They are literally "moveable feasts" that can be served immediately or parked temporarily in the freezer. Whether you put them in paper or plastic, cast iron or terra cotta, just a bow or ribbon of calico can make them look as polished and perfect as gold.

Such portable recipes are specifically suited to meet and greet those occasions when a little food for thought is much appreciated, like welcoming a new baby or next door neighbor. Compliments will go to the chef who cooks, then carries her champagne tastes with her. The casual Southwestern menu accents spinach with Veal Lasagna or Mint Dressing for salad greens. The Winter Spice Cake with buttermilk glaze stays moist and mouth-watering days after it's baked.

Office gatherings no longer have to be as staid and predictable as grey flannel and pin stripes. Bite into high tech: Spiral Sandwiches made from stuffing Armenian Cracker bread or Orzo, a pasta salad with rice texture. And if your boss is a chocolate lover, these cookies will cinch a promotion. Even the fruit centerpiece is edible, especially important to those who worry about "maximum utilization of resources". Hospitality may have left the house but not the heart. It's simply changed form to poetry in motion.

HOSPITALITY

SOUTHWESTERN WELCOME

VEAL LASAGNA
p. 10

CHICKEN SUPERB
p. 10

SALAD GREENS WITH
MINT DRESSING
p. 10

TOMATOES SOMERSET
p. 11

WINTER SPICE CAKE WITH
BUTTERMILK GLAZE
p. 11

PEANUT BUTTER SWIRL BARS
p. 11

ITALIAN BREAD

CHAMPAGNE

OFFICE WARMING

SPIRAL SANDWICHES
p. 15

ORZO PASTA SALAD
p. 14

MOCHA CHIP COOKIES
p. 15

KAHLUA BARS
p. 191

PEANUT BUTTER SPECIALS
p. 14

COCONUT MACADAMIA COOKIES
p. 14

FRUIT BASKET

HERB TEA

SOUTHWESTERN WELCOME

VEAL LASAGNA

CHICKEN SUPERB

SALAD GREENS WITH
MINT DRESSING

TOMATOES SOMERSET

ITALIAN BREAD

WINTER SPICE CAKE WITH
BUTTERMILK GLAZE

PEANUT BUTTER SWIRL BARS

CHAMPAGNE

VEAL LASAGNA

4 pounds ground veal	3 eggs, beaten
¾ cup butter, melted	1¼ pounds ricotta cheese
½ cup plus 2 Tablespoons flour	¾ cup sour cream
3¼ cups chicken broth	2 10-ounce packages frozen chopped spinach, thawed and squeezed dry
½ teaspoon salt	
¼ teaspoon white pepper	
½ teaspoon oregano	1¼ pounds Mozzarella cheese, sliced
¼ teaspoon tarragon	
1¼ teaspoons basil	½ pound spinach lasagna noodles, cooked
½ teaspoon garlic powder	
½ teaspoon thyme	1¼ cups grated Parmesan cheese
pinch sage	

Preheat oven to 350°. In a large skillet, brown veal; drain and set aside. In a large saucepan, combine butter and flour and stir over low heat for 5 to 8 minutes until flour is brown. Slowly stir in chicken broth. Add salt, pepper and herbs and cook until thick. Mix veal into sauce. In a medium bowl, combine eggs, ricotta and sour cream. To assemble, put a layer of veal sauce in bottom of a 9x13-inch baking dish. Top veal with noodles, followed by layers of ricotta mixture, spinach, Mozzarella and Parmesan. Repeat layers. Bake for 40 minutes. Cool slightly before cutting into squares. *Serves 8.*

Note: If fresh lasagna noodles are used, they do not need to be cooked before assembling dish.

CHICKEN SUPERB

4 large chicken breast halves, skinned and boned	2 cups whipping cream
	2 Tablespoons dry sherry
6 Tablespoons butter, melted	10 ounces fresh mushrooms, sliced
6 Tablespoons flour	2 Tablespoons butter, melted
2 cups chicken broth	
1½ teaspoons salt	½ cup slivered almonds, toasted
½ teaspoon celery salt	
dash Beau Monde	6 ounces medium egg noodles, cooked and drained
½ teaspoon ground marjoram	
3 Tablespoons chopped fresh parsley	½ cup grated Cheddar cheese

Preheat oven to 350°. Wrap chicken breasts in foil and bake for 1 hour. Cool and cut into large strips; set aside. In a large skillet, combine 6 Tablespoons butter and flour. Do not brown. Stirring over low heat, add broth and season with salt, celery salt, Beau Monde, marjoram and parsley. Continue to cook, stirring constantly until thickened. Add cream and sherry and set aside. In a small skillet, sauté the mushrooms in 2 Tablespoons butter. Add mushrooms and almonds to sauce. Combine sauce with chicken and noodles. Pour into casserole dish and top with cheese. Bake for 35 to 40 minutes. *Serves 6.*

MINT DRESSING

1 clove garlic	¼ cup lemon juice
1 teaspoon salt	¼ cup olive oil
3-4 springs fresh mint	

In food processor fitted with metal blade, process garlic, salt and mint. Add lemon juice and oil and mix well. Toss with salad greens to serve. *Makes ½ cup.*

TOMATOES SOMERSET

6	medium tomatoes	2	Tablespoons brown sugar
3	teaspoons minced onion	2	Tablespoons butter, melted
1	cup soft white bread crumbs		salt and pepper

Preheat oven to 375°. Cut a slice off the top of each tomato and scoop out part of the pulp. In a medium bowl, mix onion, bread crumbs, brown sugar and melted butter. Season mixture with salt and pepper to taste and stuff into tomatoes. Place in a buttered baking dish. Bake 15 to 20 minutes or until well browned. *Serves 6.*

PEANUT BUTTER SWIRL BARS

½	cup crunchy-style peanut butter	2	teaspoons vanilla
⅓	cup butter, softened	1	cup flour
¾	cup firmly packed brown sugar	1	teaspoon baking powder
¾	cup sugar	¼	teaspoon salt
2	eggs	1	12-ounce package chocolate chips

Preheat oven to 350°. In a large bowl, combine peanut butter, brown sugar and sugar beating until creamy. Gradually beat in eggs and vanilla. Blend in flour, baking powder and salt. Spread into a greased 9x13 inch baking dish. Sprinkle chocolate chips over top. Bake for 3 minutes, then remove from oven and run knife through to marbleize. Return to oven and bake 30 minutes. Cool and cut into bars. *Makes 4 dozen.*

Wine Selection: Champagne

WINTER SPICE CAKE WITH BUTTERMILK GLAZE

Cake

2	cups flour
1	teaspoon soda
½	teaspoon salt
1	teaspoon cinnamon
1	teaspoon allspice
2	cups sugar
1	cup oil
3	eggs
1	cup buttermilk
1	cup chopped pecans
1	cup chopped dried prunes

Buttermilk Glaze

1	cup sugar
½	cup buttermilk
1	teaspoon vanilla
1	Tablespoon butter
1	Tablespoon light corn syrup
¼	teaspoon soda
¼	teaspoon salt

To prepare cake: Preheat oven to 350°. In a medium bowl, combine flour, soda, salt, cinnamon and allspice. In another large bowl, cream sugar, oil and eggs. Add half of flour mixture, then buttermilk followed by remaining flour mixture. Stir in pecans and prunes. Pour into greased and floured 10-inch Bundt cake pan. Bake for 1 hour and 10 minutes. Remove cake from pan and pour glaze over warm cake. *Serves 16.*

To prepare glaze: Combine all ingredients in small saucepan. Boil 4 to 5 minutes, stirring constantly (glaze will turn caramel color).

OFFICE WARMING

SPIRAL SANDWICHES

ORZO PASTA SALAD

FRUIT BASKET

MOCHA CHIP COOKIES

KAHLUA BARS

PEANUT BUTTER SPECIALS

COCONUT MACADAMIA COOKIES

HERB TEA

ORZO PASTA SALAD

Salad   **Dressing**

1½ cups orzo (rice-shaped   1   egg yolk
    pasta)   2   Tablespoons white wine
¼   cup olive oil   vinegar
1   9-ounce package frozen   2   teaspoons Dijon
    artichoke hearts   mustard
½   cup chicken broth   ½   cup olive oil
¼   pound prosciutto,   salt
    slivered   pepper
½   cup grated Parmesan   4   fresh basil leaves,
    cheese   chopped
3   Tablespoons fresh
    lemon juice
½   cup chopped fresh
    parsley
4   green onions (green
    and white parts), sliced
chopped fresh basil

To prepare salad: In a medium saucepan, cook orzo in boiling salted water for 7 to 10 minutes to al dente stage. Drain, rinse in cold water and drain again. Toss orzo with ¼ cup olive oil and set aside. In a small saucepan, simmer artichoke hearts in chicken broth for 6 to 8 minutes until tender. Drain, slice artichoke hearts and add to orzo. Mix in prosciutto, Parmesan, lemon juice, parsley and onions. Toss with dressing and chill at least 4 hours before serving. To serve, mix well and garnish with chopped fresh basil.

To prepare dressing: Whisk together egg yolk, vinegar, mustard, olive oil, basil and salt and pepper to taste. *Serves 6.*

Note: Can be prepared 1-2 days in advance.

PEANUT BUTTER SPECIALS

1   cup crunchy-style   1   cup butter, melted
    peanut butter   1   cup powdered sugar
1½ cups graham cracker   2   cups milk chocolate
    crumbs   chips

In a large bowl, mix peanut butter, graham cracker crumbs, butter and sugar. Pat firmly into a 9x9-inch dish and chill until hard. Melt chocolate in top of double boiler over simmering water and spread on top of peanut butter mixture. Return to refrigerator and chill until hard. To serve, bring to room temperature and slice into squares. *Makes 2 dozen.*

COCONUT MACADAMIA COOKIES

1   cup flour   1   teaspoon vanilla
½   teaspoon baking   ½   cup quick cooking or
    powder   regular oats
½   teaspoon salt   1⅓ cups grated coconut
½   teaspoon baking soda   ⅔ cups additional grated
½   cup butter or   coconut
    margarine   ½   cup Macadamia nuts,
½   cup sugar   chopped
½   cup brown sugar
1   egg

Preheat oven to 375°. Mix flour, baking powder, salt and soda in a small bowl. In a large bowl, cream butter gradually adding both sugars until dough is light and fluffy. Blend in egg and vanilla. Stir in flour mixture, oats, nuts and 1⅓ cups coconut. Drop from teaspoon onto greased cookie sheets and sprinkle with remaining coconut. Bake for 10 minutes until golden brown. *Makes 4 dozen cookies.*

SPIRAL SANDWICHES

1   15-inch Armenian cracker bread
1   3-ounce package cream cheese, softened
1   Tablespoon chopped fresh basil (or 1 teaspoon dried)
1   Tablespoon chopped fresh oregano (or 1 teaspoon dried)
¼   teaspoon garlic powder
seasoned salt, to taste

¼   pound smoked ham, thinly sliced
1   large tomato, thinly sliced and blotted dry
4   thin slices Monterey Jack cheese
½   cup alfalfa sprouts
2   large romaine lettuce leaves

Quickly run cold water completely over both sides of cracker bread. Place between damp towel, sesame seed side down, and let rest for 1 hour until soft enough to roll without splitting. Season cream cheese with basil, oregano, garlic powder and seasoned salt to taste. Leaving the cracker bread on bottom towel, spread the seasoned cream cheese to cover. Place ham over the cream cheese followed by tomatoes, then cheese. Sprinkle sprouts over layers. Place lettuce across the bottom of cracker bread. With the aid of the towel, starting where the leaves are, roll the cracker bread like a jelly roll as tightly as possible. Wrap roll in plastic wrap and refrigerate for 2-3 hours (up to 24 hours). To serve, cut off uneven pieces. *Serves 3-4.*

Note: For variations, use combinations of cream cheese, dill, chutney, smoked turkey, Brie, chopped parsley, fresh spinach, Saga bleu cheese, prosciutto and basil leaves.

MOCHA CHIP COOKIES

3   cups chocolate chips
8   Tablespoons unsalted butter
4   ounces unsweetened chocolate
½   cup flour
½   teaspoon baking powder

½   teaspoon salt
4   eggs, room temperature
1½ cups sugar
1½ Tablespoons instant coffee
2   teaspoons vanilla
2   cups toasted chopped pecans

Preheat oven to 375°. Melt 1½ cups chocolate chips, butter and unsweetened chocolate in top of double boiler over simmering water. In a small bowl, combine flour, baking powder and salt. In a large bowl, beat eggs, sugar, instant coffee and vanilla for 2 minutes with an electric mixer on high speed. Stir in chocolate mixture, then flour mixture and combine thoroughly. Add 1½ cups chocolate chips and pecans. Drop onto cookie sheets lined with foil and bake for 8 minutes. Do not overbake. Cool completely before removing from cookie sheets. *Makes 5 dozen.*

Note: Cracked and shiny in appearance.

CULINARY QUILT

CULINARY QUILT

Cooks often make the history books when guests dine on adventure. Start a new revolution in your kitchen. If you banquet on rice, peppers, garlic and spices, basic foods frequently found East and West, don't forget to experiment with surprises like cactus pear and cloud ear, tomatillos and chestnuts. Take risks!

Whether good food comes from the next county or way beyond our border, it's part of our constitution to adopt what we like. Who thought it or bought it makes no difference. We may talk Texan but we speak any language when it translates to tasty cuisine.

We see our community as a quilt of culinary bits and pieces, a patchwork of taste and traditions. The influence of Spanish and Oriental foods is symbolic of the combination of cultures in our city's history. And some of the best is when East meets West.

We may have won our independence from Mexico a sesquicentennial ago, but we forgot to tell our taste buds. Tex-Mex is our regional fare, and you don't have to cross the Rio Grande for a "Fiesta" menu that clicks better than castenets. Olé for our Steak Adobe that's served with a cheese and chili sauce. Greenhorns can opt for a less "caliente" pepper if they por favor. And our jalapeños won't be doing the Mexican hot dance either as they are stuffed with salmon for a milder flavor. With the Ceviche, invest only in blue chips (blue tortilla chips that is), from the state of New Mexico.

If you would rather introduce your guests to the "Flavors of the Orient," here's a menu that's not just "so so" but definitely "ah so". The sauces and spices of the ancient world should no longer be locked up with the wok in the closet. Gone are the days of soy and La Choy! This is the year of the lamb, cooked crispy, Hunan style. Instead of egg rolls for appetizer, try our more daring Chicken and Pork Oriental. And our Fried Rice, a primavera version with spinach, will receive more "goshes" than the Great Wall. It all sounds so good we may eat our words.

CULINARY QUILT

FIESTA

CEVICHE
p. 24

STUFFED JALAPEÑOS
p. 24

TORTILLA SOUP
p. 24

STEAK ADOBE
p. 145

GREEN CHICKEN
ENCHILADAS
p. 25

PICO DE GALLO
p. 25

AVOCADO SALAD
p. 134

PRALINES
p. 25

TEQUILA FRUIT DIP
p. 25

RUM PUNCH
p. 25

FLAVORS OF THE ORIENT

CHICKEN AND PORK ORIENTAL
p. 28

SESAME ASPARAGUS SALAD
p. 28

CHICKEN AND PEPPERS HOISIN
p. 29

CHILI PRAWNS
p. 28

HUNAN LAMB
p. 140

FRIED RICE WITH SPINACH
p. 182

KIWI FRUIT WITH ALMONDS
p. 29

MINT SHERBET
p. 29

Fiesta

Ceviche

Stuffed Jalapeños

Tortilla Soup

Steak Adobe

Green Chicken
Enchiladas

Pico de Gallo

Avocado Salad

Pralines

Tequila Fruit Dip

Rum Punch

Tortilla Soup

2 Tablespoons safflower oil	1 quart chicken stock
1 large onion, quartered	1 quart beef stock
8 tomatoes	6 ounces tomato sauce
2 Tablespoons safflower oil	salt
	cayenne or black pepper
1 corn tortilla, chopped	2 cooked chicken breasts, chopped
4 cloves garlic, minced	
1 ancho chili, stemmed, seeded, toasted and finely chopped	4 ounces Cheddar or Monterey Jack cheese, grated
1 bay leaf	1 avocado, diced
1 sprig dried epasote (optional)	2 cups thinly sliced, fried tortillas
2 teaspoons ground cumin	sprigs of fresh cilantro

Preheat oven to broil. Rub onions and tomatoes with oil. Place on cookie sheet and broil 4 to 6 inches from heat until charred on all sides. Put tomatoes and onions in food processor fitted with metal blade or blender and process until smooth. Set aside. Heat remaining 2 Tablespoons oil in Dutch oven. Add tortilla, garlic and ancho chili. Sauté for 3 to 4 minutes. Add bay leaf, epasote, cumin, chicken and beef stocks. Heat to a boil. Stir in the tomato-onion mixture and tomato sauce. Simmer over medium heat for 30 minutes. Add salt and pepper to taste. Strain through a coarse strainer. (Soup may be prepared ahead to this point and reheated when ready to serve.) To serve, put warm cooked chicken, cheese, avocado and crisp tortillas in bowls. Heat the broth to a boil and ladle over chicken. Garnish with cilantro. *Serves 8.*

Ceviche

1 pound fresh bass, crappie or catfish, cut into ½ - inch pieces	½ cup chopped black olives
lime juice	½ cup tomato juice
	⅓ cup olive oil
3-4 jalapeño peppers, seeded and chopped	2 cloves garlic, minced
2 medium onions, chopped	½ teaspoon thyme
	½ teaspoon oregano
2 tomatoes, peeled and chopped	1 Tablespoon parsley
	salt and pepper
1 3-ounce can whole green chilies, chopped	

In a large bowl, marinate fish in lime juice to cover. Cover overnight at room temperature. In another large bowl, mix remaining ingredients. Cover and chill overnight. Blot fish dry and add to vegetable mixture. Chill 2-3 hours before serving. *Serves 8-10.*

Stuffed Jalapeños

1 pound mild Cheddar cheese, grated	1 Tablespoon instant onion flakes
6 hard boiled eggs, chopped	salt
mayonnaise	1 Tablespoon chopped fresh parsley
1 15-ounce can red salmon	2 pound can whole jalapeños
2 Tablespoons lemon juice	paprika

In a large bowl, moisten cheese and eggs with mayonnaise. Remove bones and skin from salmon and flake. Add salmon, lemon juice, onion, salt and parsley to cheese mixture with enough additional mayonnaise to hold it all together. Rinse jalapeños under cold running water. Split each pepper in half, lengthwise and remove the seeds under running water. Drain on paper towels. Stuff salmon mixture generously into each jalapeño. Sprinkle with paprika and chill. *Serves 20.*

Green Chicken Enchiladas

4   chicken breast halves,
    cooked, deboned and
    cut in 1-inch pieces
1   8-ounce package
    cream cheese,
    softened
1   small onion, finely
    chopped
salt
1   pound tomatillas
1   cup water
1   4-ounce can green
    salsa
1   cup whipping cream
15-18 corn tortillas
2   Tablespoons oil
8   ounces grated
    Monterey Jack cheese

Preheat oven to 350°. In a large bowl, mix chicken, cream cheese and onion. Season to taste with salt and set aside. In a large saucepan, cook tomatillas in water over low heat until tender about 10 minutes. Cool, drain, then liquefy in blender for approximately one minute. Transfer to medium bowl. Add salsa and cream. Whisk until well blended. Set aside. In a medium skillet, soften tortillas in hot oil. Drain well. Place one Tablespoon tomatilla sauce in a tortilla with 1 Tablespoon chicken mixture. Roll and place in 9x13-inch baking dish, seam side down. Repeat with remaining tortillas. Pour remaining sauce over enchiladas and top with grated cheese. Bake for 30 minutes. *Serves 6 to 8.*

Pico De Gallo

2   large tomatoes, finely
    chopped
1   medium onion, chopped
2   cloves garlic, minced
2-3 fresh jalapeño peppers,
    finely chopped
2   Tablespoons chopped
    cilantro
1   Tablespoon lime juice
1   Tablespoon olive oil
salt

In a large bowl, combine all ingredients and season to taste with salt. Refrigerate for at least one hour. Best if chilled overnight before serving. *Makes 2 cups.*

Pralines

2   cups sugar
1   teaspoon baking soda
1   cup buttermilk
2   Tablespoons butter
2   cups pecan halves

In a large saucepan, combine sugar, soda and buttermilk. Bring to a boil over low heat and cook until mixture reaches 210° on a candy thermometer, about 5 minutes. Add butter and pecan halves and continue cooking until mixture reaches soft ball stage (234°). Remove from heat and stir with a wooden spoon until cool. Drop by teaspoon onto waxed paper, adding warm water if the mixture gets too thick. *Makes 2 dozen.*

Tequila Fruit Dip

2   cups sour cream
3   Tablespoons sugar
3   Tablespoons tequila
1   Tablespoon grated lime
    zest
1   Tablespoon grated
    orange zest
1/4 teaspoon cinnamon
3   Tablespoons ground
    almonds
orange and lime zest
    for garnish

Combine all ingredients in a medium bowl and whisk until well blended. Cover and chill several hours. Best if chilled overnight. Garnish with zest. Serve with fresh fruit. *Makes 2½ cups.*

Rum Punch

12 ounces frozen limeade
    concentrate, thawed
1½ cups fresh orange juice
1½ cups dark rum
1½ cups light rum
1½ cups water (or to taste)

In a large pitcher, mix all ingredients. Chill up to 24 hours. To serve, pour over ice and garnish with lime slices. *Serves 8.*

FLAVORS OF
THE ORIENT

CHICKEN AND PORK ORIENTAL

SESAME ASPARAGUS SALAD

CHICKEN AND PEPPERS HOISIN

CHILI PRAWNS

HUNAN LAMB

FRIED RICE WITH SPINACH

KIWI FRUIT WITH ALMONDS

MINT SHERBET

CHICKEN AND PORK ORIENTAL

8	dried Chinese mushrooms	2	Tablespoons soy sauce
½	cup warm water	2	Tablespoons oyster sauce
4	Tablespoons peanut or vegetable oil	½	teaspoon sugar
3	whole scallions, finely chopped	2	teaspoons cornstarch
1	teaspoon finely chopped ginger root	2	Tablespoons cold water or chicken broth
1	pound freshly ground pork	1½-2	cups Hoisin sauce
1	pound freshly ground white meat chicken	8-10	large romaine lettuce leaves
½	cup coarsely chopped water chestnuts		

In a small bowl, soak mushrooms in ½ cup water for 30 minutes. Drain mushrooms, reserving ¼ cup water. Heat a wok or skillet over high heat for 30 seconds. Add oil, swirl and heat an additional 30 seconds. Stir in scallions and ginger, then add both meats. Stir-fry 2-4 minutes. Mix in mushrooms, chestnuts, soy, oyster sauce and sugar. Stir in reserved water and cook 1 minute. In a small bowl, dissolve cornstarch in broth. Add to wok and stir constantly until all ingredients are coated with a light, clear glaze. Transfer mixture to a platter. To serve, thin Hoisin with chicken broth if desired and thinly spread on a lettuce leaf. Place 2 Tablespoons meat mixture over Hoisin. Roll up lengthwise, tucking in one end as it is rolled. *Serves 8 as a first course.*

SESAME ASPARAGUS SALAD

2	pounds fresh asparagus, sliced in 2-inch pieces	½	teaspoon white wine vinegar
1½	Tablespoons soy sauce	2	green onions (green part), chopped
1	teaspoon sugar	1-2	Tablespoons sesame seeds, toasted
2	teaspoons sesame oil		

In a large saucepan, steam asparagus until tender, 2 to 3 minutes, then plunge immediately into ice water to set color. Drain. In a small bowl, combine soy sauce, sugar, sesame oil and vinegar. Toss asparagus with soy mixture and chill no longer than 2 hours. To serve, sprinkle with onions and sesame seeds. *Serves 8.*

CHILI PRAWNS

3	Tablespoons peanut oil	1½	Tablespoons Worcestershire sauce
1	teaspoon ginger, chopped finely	1½	Tablespoons soy sauce
¼	cup green onion	2	Tablespoons water
16	large fresh prawns or shrimp, peeled, deveined and halved crosswise	2	small red chili peppers, chopped (or to taste)
3	Tablespoons sherry	¼	cup chopped green onion(green part)
2	Tablespoons tomato sauce		

In a large skillet, heat oil over high heat. Sauté ginger and ¼ cup green onion for 30 seconds. Add prawns and sauté for 2-3 minutes. Stir in sherry, tomato sauce, Worcestershire sauce, soy sauce, water and chili peppers (use fewer chili peppers or omit for a less spicy flavor). Reduce heat to medium-high and cook, stirring constantly until sauce thickens, about 2 minutes. Garnish with ¼ cup chopped green onion and serve immediately. *Serves 4.*

CHICKEN AND PEPPERS HOISIN

2 cups boneless, skinless,
   chicken cut in 1-inch strips
2 cups oil
¾ cup pecan halves
1 green bell pepper, cut
   in 1-inch cubes
1 red bell pepper, cut in
   1-inch cubes
salt

Marinade		Hoisin sauce	
2	teaspoons chopped garlic	½	Tablespoon sugar
2	Tablespoons sherry	½	Tablespoon vinegar
2	Tablespoons cornstarch	¼	cup chicken stock
2	Tablespoons soy sauce	1	Tablespoon soy sauce
½	teaspoon salt	1	Tablespoon cornstarch
1	egg white		

To prepare marinade: In a medium bowl, combine garlic, sherry, cornstarch, soy sauce, salt and egg white. Toss in chicken pieces and marinate at least 20 minutes.

To prepare chicken: In a wok or large skillet, heat oil on medium high heat and fry pecans for 1½ to 2 minutes. Remove pecans and set aside. Pour oil into jar. Add 2 Tablespoons of oil back to skillet and quickly stir-fry the peppers, adding a dash of salt. Add 4-5 Tablespoons reserved oil to skillet and stir fry chicken cubes until meat turns white. Remove chicken pieces and peppers and discard oil.

To prepare sauce: In a small bowl, combine sugar, vinegar, stock, soy sauce and cornstarch. Heat 1 Tablespoon oil in skillet over medium high heat. Add sauce and cook for 30 seconds. Add chicken, peppers and pecans. Stir fry until heated thoroughly. *Serves 4.*

KIWI FRUIT WITH ALMONDS

1	cup water	3-4 Tablespoons Kirsch
½	cup sugar	½ cup sliced almonds,
1	cinnamon stick	toasted
2-3	drops vanilla	whipped cream
10	kiwis, peeled and sliced	

In a small saucepan, combine water, sugar and cinnamon. Bring mixture to a boil and simmer 3 to 4 minutes. Cool syrup and add vanilla. Chill. Soak kiwis in Kirsch, then coat with syrup. To serve, spoon fruit into dessert bowls and garnish with almonds and whipped cream. *Serves 6-8.*

MINT SHERBET

2	lemons	1	large bunch mint, finely chopped
2	oranges		
	grated zest of 1 lemon		green food coloring
2	cups water	1	egg white, lightly beaten (not stiff)
2	cups sugar		

Juice lemons and oranges. Combine with lemon zest in a large bowl. In a medium saucepan, combine water and sugar. Cook over medium high heat for 10 minutes until sugar is dissolved. Place mint in a medium bowl and pour hot syrup over mixture. Steep mint mixture for 1 hour. Strain mint mixture into fruit juices and add 1-2 drops of green food coloring. When cool, add egg white. Cover mixture and freeze until firm, about 6-8 hours. Stir mixture once during freezing process. *Serves 6.*

Wine Selection: White Zinfandel

SPORTING LIFE

SPORTING LIFE

Cheering on your favorite team is just as much a sport in Dallas as the game itself. To keep in strong voice and high spirits, fans love to snack. Whether you serve your guests "pick-up" (from the back of the truck) or "take-out" (out at the stadium or out by the TV room), be prepared for a feast. If you prefer to organize ahead, wrap up a box lunch in tissue, brightly-colored to match your team.

Dallas sports fans aren't necessarily the best sports. We will "rah, rah","yee, hah" and argue the extra point well into the wee hours of the morning. We play to win whether in a stadium, on the tennis court, a polo field or a fairway. We also love to tout and toot about our very own teams, the Cowboys, Mavericks and Rangers, not to mention Texas alma maters like SMU, UT and TCU.

"Take us out to the ballgame" is a familiar refrain in this town, but forget the peanuts and crackerjacks. We want no concessions when it comes to food. For a sporting event that's not only a hit but a homerun, we recommend a Texas Tailgate party. Serving specialties from the back of the Wagoneer is a great way to gather friends for a welcome time-out from clean-up in the kitchen. You can cook creatively for these occasions and still not send your game plan into overtime.

We've stuffed the Pecan Cheese Spread into a small carved pumpkin, ripe and right for fall decoration. If there is a hunter (or golfer) in the family, have him bring home a birdie for the Pita Bread with Wild Game Picadillo. Have you ever heard of brown bagging a pie? Ours comes baked in one and brown sugar as well. And if you're not driving, wash it all down with your favorite Texas beer. You'll be ready to sing the fight song on key.

Our version of the Box Lunch comes in a basket that fits perfectly onto a lap or in a budget. We've tackled some unusual recipes that are not par for the course but travel well and taste terrific. Pesto Stuffed Chicken guarantees any cook a winner. You'll have to referee the seconds on the Orange-Apricot Muffins and for scoring touchdowns, a super bowl of Fusilli Pasta with Aioli Sauce can't be beat. We hope these menus and suggestions will lighten your kitchen quarterbacking duty so all you need to worry about before the game is who has the tickets.

SPORTING LIFE

TAILGATE

PECAN CHEESE SPREAD
WITH CHIPS
p. 38

WILD GAME PICADILLO IN
PITA BREAD
p. 38

COLD AVOCADO AND GREEN
CHILI SOUP
p. 38

POPPY SEED CHICKEN SALAD
WITH APRICOTS
p. 38

GREEK TOMATO SALAD
p. 39

PEAR PIE
p. 39

OATMEAL SESAME COOKIES
p. 39

BEER WITH LIME

BOX LUNCH

PESTO STUFFED CHICKEN
BREASTS
p. 42

FUSILLI PASTA SALAD WITH
SUNDRIED TOMATOES AND
AIOLI SAUCE
p. 43

ORANGE APRICOT MUFFINS
p. 42

ICED BRANDY BROWNIES
p. 43

RED GRAPES

TAILGATE

Pecan Cheese Spread
With Chips

Wild Game Picadillo In
Pita Bread

Cold Avocado And Green
Chili Soup

Poppy Seed Chicken Salad
With Apricots

Greek Tomato Salad

Pear Pie

Oatmeal Sesame Cookies

Beer With Lime

PECAN CHEESE SPREAD

2	cups firmly packed grated Cheddar cheese	2	Tablespoons chopped green onions
¾	cup mayonnaise	4	strips bacon, cooked and crumbled
½	cup chopped pecans		

In a small bowl, combine ingredients. Chill 12 hours. Serve with crackers or garlic bagel chips. *Serves 8.*

WILD GAME PICADILLO IN PITA BREAD HALVES

1	Tablespoon oil	¾	cup tomatoes, peeled and chopped
1	pound ground venison or any other game	1	teaspoon salt
1	clove garlic, minced	½	teaspoon cinnamon
½	yellow onion, chopped	½	teaspoon cumin
1	small apple, peeled, cored and diced	¼	cup seedless raisins or currants
¼	cup beef broth	⅓	cup almonds, thinly sliced
1	Tablespoon vinegar		

In a large skillet, sauté ground meat, garlic and onion in 1 Tablespoon oil over medium heat until browned. Add apple, broth, vinegar, tomatoes, salt, cinnamon and cumin; continue to simmer, stirring occasionally or until liquid is absorbed. Remove from heat and stir in raisins and almonds. Serve in pita bread halves. *Serves 8-10.*

Note: Add slices of avocado and sour cream in pita bread halves. Substitute flour tortillas for pita bread halves. Serve picadillo in omelettes or baked in roasted, peeled chilies or bell peppers.

POPPY SEED CHICKEN SALAD WITH APRICOTS

½	cup chopped almonds, toasted	½	teaspoon grated lemon peel
½	cup lemon juice	½	cup dried apricots
½	cup salad oil	4	cups chopped cooked chicken (2 pounds)
2	Tablespoons honey	1	red apple, cored and thinly sliced
2	Tablespoons Dijon mustard		
2	Tablespoons poppy seeds	salt	
½	cup sliced green onion tops		

Preheat oven to 350°. Toast almonds until browned, set aside. In a medium bowl, mix lemon juice, oil, honey, mustard, poppy seeds, onions and lemon peel. Add apricots; let stand at least 30 minutes. Add chicken to dressing mixture. Before serving, toss with apple slices and almonds. Salt to taste. *Serves 6.*

Note: Dressing mixture may be made a day in advance.

COLD AVOCADO AND GREEN CHILI SOUP

1	ripe avocado, pitted, peeled and quartered	1	cup sour cream
1	4-ounce can green chilies, drained	½	teaspoon salt
1	tomatillo, quartered	⅛	teaspoon white pepper
2	cups chicken stock, chilled	2	corn tortillas
		¼	cup peanut oil

Cut tortillas into 2x¼-inch strips and fry in peanut oil heated to 375°. Set aside. In a blender, combine avocado, chilies, tomatillo and chicken stock at high speed until smooth. Add sour cream, salt and pepper. Blend well. Garnish with tortilla strips and serve immediately. *Serves 8.*

GREEK TOMATO SALAD

Salad

6 medium ripe tomatoes, cubed
8 ounces feta or cream cheese, cubed
½ cup Greek or ripe olives

Dressing

3 Tablespoons olive oil
1½ Tablespoons lemon juice
1 small clove garlic, crushed
1½ teaspoons oregano, crushed
½ teaspoon salt
⅛ teaspoon black pepper

To prepare salad: Place tomatoes in a medium bowl with cheese and olives. Toss with dressing. Serve immediately. *Serves 8.*

To prepare dressing: Combine olive oil, lemon juice, garlic, oregano, salt and pepper. Allow flavors to blend for 10 minutes.

PEAR PIE

1 9 - inch unbaked pie shell

Filling

4-5 cups pears, peeled and sliced
1 lemon
½ cup sugar
2½ Tablespoons flour
¼ teaspoon nutmeg

Topping

8 Tablespoons butter, softened
½ cup dark brown sugar
½ cup flour

To prepare filling: Preheat oven to 425°. In a medium bowl, squeeze the juice of one lemon over sliced pears. Set aside. In a small bowl, combine sugar, flour and nutmeg. Sprinkle this mixture over pears to coat. Arrange pears in unbaked pie shell.

To prepare topping: Cream butter, brown sugar and flour. Spread over pear mixture in pie shell.

Insert pie pan into brown paper bag, fold edge, fasten securely to create a vacuum. Place on cookie sheet and bake for 1 hour. *Serves 8.*

OATMEAL SESAME COOKIES

¾ cup butter
2 cups sugar
2 eggs, beaten
2 cups flour
2 cups old-fashioned oatmeal
1 teaspoon vanilla
1 Tablespoon cinnamon
1 Tablespoon ground cloves
¼ teaspoon salt
1 Tablespoon nutmeg
2 Tablespoons water
½ teaspoon soda
1 cup chopped pecans
⅓ cup sesame seeds, toasted

Preheat oven to 350°. In a large mixing bowl, cream butter and sugar; add eggs, mixing well. Add flour, oatmeal, vanilla, cinnamon, cloves, nutmeg and salt, mixing well after each addition. Stir in water and soda to form dough; add pecans and sesame seeds. Drop from spoon onto greased cookie sheets. Bake for 15 minutes or until light brown. *Makes 8 dozen.*

BOX LUNCH

PESTO STUFFED CHICKEN
BREASTS

FUSILLI PASTA SALAD WITH
SUNDRIED TOMATOES AND
AIOLI SAUCE

ORANGE APRICOT MUFFINS

ICED BRANDY BROWNIES

RED GRAPES

PESTO STUFFED CHICKEN BREASTS

Filling

1/4 cup pine nuts
1 pound fresh spinach
2 Tablespoons unsalted butter, melted
3 medium shallots, finely chopped
1/2 cup ricotta cheese
1/4 cup Pesto Sauce
1 egg yolk
1/8 teaspoon black pepper
1/2 teaspoon seasoning salt

4 slices prosciutto, 1/8 inch thick, halved
4 large whole chicken breasts, skinned, boned, halved, and flattened
3 Tablespoons unsalted butter, melted
3 Tablespoons fresh lemon juice
additional Pesto Sauce
4 Tablespoons mayonnaise

Pesto Sauce

1/4 cup pine nuts
3 cloves garlic
2 cups fresh basil leaves
1/2 teaspoon salt
1/2 cup olive oil
1/2 cup grated Parmesan cheese

To prepare filling. Preheat oven to 350°. Toast nuts in oven for 5 minutes; set aside. In 10-inch skillet, steam spinach over medium heat for 2 minutes. Remove from heat; drain. Rinse in cold water to stop cooking process. Place spinach in dry towel and squeeze until all excess liquid is gone. Chop medium-fine. In small skillet, sauté shallots in butter over low heat; set aside. In a large bowl, combine nuts, spinach, shallots, cheese, Pesto, yolk, pepper and salt.

To prepare Pesto Sauce: In food processor fitted with steel blade, process nuts and garlic until paste-like. Add basil and salt. With machine running, pour olive oil in thin stream through feed tube; process until blended. Chill. Before using, blend in Parmesan. (Can be frozen before adding cheese. Can be served on pasta or vegetables.) *Makes 1 cup.*

To assemble: Preheat oven to 375°. Place half slice prosciutto on each pounded chicken breast. Spread filling evenly over prosciutto. Beginning with small end, roll up chicken. Place chicken rolls seam down in a greased medium baking dish. In a small bowl mix lemon juice and butter; spoon over chicken. Bake 20-25 minutes, basting with pan juices. Chill. To serve, slice chicken. Lighten remaining pesto sauce with mayonnaise and serve with chicken. *Serves 4-6.*

ORANGE-APRICOT MUFFINS

Muffins

2 cups flour
1 teaspoon baking soda
1 1/2 cups sugar
2 eggs
1 cup sour milk or buttermilk
1/2 cup butter, melted

1/2 cup grated orange rind
1/2 cup chopped dried apricots
1 cup chopped pecans

Glaze

1 Tablespoon sugar
juice of 2 medium oranges

To prepare muffins: Preheat oven to 375°. In a large mixing bowl, sift together flour, soda and sugar. Stir in eggs, milk and butter (do not beat). Add rind, fruit and nuts. Spoon 1 Tablespoon batter into greased small muffin tins. Bake 15 minutes. Meanwhile, prepare glaze by combining juice and sugar. Immediately pour 1 teaspoon glaze over each hot muffin. Serve warm. *Makes 5 dozen.*

FUSILLI PASTA SALAD WITH SUN-DRIED TOMATOES AND AIOLI SAUCE

Aioli Sauce

10 large cloves garlic
1 Tablespoon stale bread crumbs
¼ cup white wine vinegar
1 egg yolk
1 cup olive oil
1 teaspoon Dijon mustard
½ teaspoon Tabasco sauce

Salad

1 pound fusilli pasta, cooked
2 6½-ounce jars marinated artichoke hearts, do not drain
1¼ cups Aioli Sauce
¼ cup chopped sun-dried tomatoes, chopped
¾ teaspoon salt
½ teaspoon black pepper
1 cup frozen peas, thawed
cayenne pepper
romaine lettuce leaves
parsley
1 lemon, cut into 8 wedges

To prepare sauce: In food processor fitted with steel blade, mince garlic. Add crumbs, vinegar and yolk. Process until smooth. With machine running, add olive oil in a steady stream through feed tube. Transfer to a small bowl; whisk in mustard and Tabasco.

To prepare salad: In a large bowl, toss pasta, artichoke hearts with marinade, sauce, tomatoes, salt and pepper. Chill 12 hours. To serve, toss pasta with peas. Line salad bowl with lettuce; mound pasta mixture in center. Sprinkle with cayenne; garnish with parsley and lemon. *Serves 8.*

Wine Selection: Fall Creek Blanc de Blanc

ICED BRANDY BROWNIES

Brownies

¾ cup sifted flour
¼ teaspoon baking powder
¼ teaspoon salt
⅓ cup honey
2 Tablespoons coffee
½ cup butter, room temperature
6 ounces semisweet chocolate, chopped
1 teaspoon vanilla
2 eggs
1½ cups pecans, chopped
2 Tablespoons brandy

Icing

½ cup butter, softened
1 teaspoon vanilla
2 cups confectioner's sugar, sifted

Chocolate Topping

3 ounces semisweet chocolate
1½ Tablespoons water
2 Tablespoons butter

To prepare brownies: Preheat oven to 325°. Grease a 9x9-inch baking pan. Sift flour, baking powder and salt together. In a medium saucepan over moderate heat, combine coffee, honey, butter and chocolate. Stir until melted. Remove from heat and stir in vanilla. Add the eggs one at a time mixing well after each addition. Add flour mixture and beat until smooth. Stir in nuts and pour into prepared pan. Bake for 25 minutes. Remove from oven and brush brandy over hot cake. Cool completely. Spread icing over cake, smoothing the top. Chill until icing is set. Drizzle chocolate topping decoratively over icing and chill to set before cutting into bars. *Makes 18.*

To prepare icing: In the small bowl of electric mixer, beat butter. Add vanilla and gradually add sugar beating until soft and fluffy. Spread over cooled brownies.

To prepare topping: Combine ingredients in the top of a double boiler over simmering water and stir occasionally until melted. Drizzle over iced brownies.

TRADITIONS

TRADITIONS

Any tradition, no matter how seemingly insignificant, will provide memories not only for your family but also for your friends. If your children are old enough, let them supervise the adults. Paste valentines, dye eggs, carve pumpkins, pull taffy, bake gingerbread, ice cookies, hang wishbones or hum hymns. Nothing shares better than time, laughter and life's simpler moments.

Texans didn't start their traditions from scratch. The customs and cultures of the immigrants who settled here scattered over the land like bluebonnets. These first Texans handed down traditions, but never as hand-me-downs. They valued ingenuity and individuality. Today we're making folklore in our own way, as homemade and handmade as yesterday.

There are no lone stars when it comes to celebrating the "Fourth of July". O say, can you see the patriots of the Park Cities bike parade down Preston Road each year in honor of Uncle Sam. They, like most citizens of this city, love a parade and a picnic. Be the home of the brave, fly the flag above the grill and let the neighborhood congregate.

Grill the ears of corn in their shucks and add cumin for a new fangled, star spangled taste. And for real dessert sparklers, we think Lemon Sherbert, Grape Ice Cream and Praline Ice Cream are three homemade flavors that complement each other as perfectly as red, white and blue.

Our best intentions to entertain evaporate as quickly as shopping days before Christmas. But our "Holiday Brunch" can be simple. For a Texas Christmas, deck your halls with greenery like arborvitae, juniper, magnolia or mistletoe. Ornament your home with gifts from nature: a grapevine, bird's nest, pine cones, symbols of a simpler time. For your surprise package, slice a fruit that's not just fresh but less frequently used, like star fruit, kiwi or pomegranate. And for a garnish that looks fancy and frosty, dip grapes in egg whites and sprinkle with sugar. Even the appetites of the diet conscious will thaw! Just as photographs are added to the family album, save a few new or favorite recipes each year. Originals soon become traditionals!

TRADITIONS

FOURTH OF JULY

JALAPEÑO BLACK-EYED PEA DIP
p. 52

SPICY GRILLED SHRIMP
p. 52

MARINATED CHICKEN SKEWERS
p. 52

RAINBOW RICE
p. 182

GRILLED CORN WITH
CHILI BUTTER
p. 172

RED PEPPER AND
PAPAYA RELISH
p. 522

POPPY SEED CHEESE BREAD
p. 53

HONEY COOKIES
p. 53

LEMON SHERBET
p. 53

GRAPE ICE CREAM
p. 53

PRALINE ICE CREAM
p. 55

HOLIDAY BRUNCH

SAUSAGE FILLED CREPES WITH
DILL SAUCE
p. 142

FRENCH CUSTARD TOAST
p. 58

SCRAMBLED EGGS MAGDA
p. 57

CRANBERRY BANANA BREAD
p. 57

HOT BUTTER MUFFINS
p. 56

LEMON PUFF COFFEE CAKE
p. 57

ORANGE STICKY BUNS
p. 56

FRESH FRUIT WITH JAMAICA SAUCE
p. 101

Fourth Of July

Jalapeño Black-eyed Pea Dip

Spicy Grilled Shrimp

Marinated Chicken Skewers

Rainbow Rice

Grilled Corn With
Chili Butter

Red Pepper And
Papaya Relish

Poppy Seed Cheese Bread

Honey Cookies

Lemon Sherbet

Grape Ice Cream

Praline Ice Cream

Lemonade

RED PEPPER AND PAPAYA RELISH

3   cups cider vinegar
1   cup sugar
2   yellow onions, thinly sliced
1½ teaspoons salt
6   red bell peppers, roasted, peeled and sliced

2   jalapeño chilies, stemmed, seeded and diced into ⅛-inch strips
2   fresh papayas or mangoes, peeled, seeded and cut in strips
    black pepper

In a 2-quart saucepan, mix vinegar and sugar. Bring to a boil. Add onions and salt. Immediately remove from heat. Let stand 15 minutes. Mix in peppers and chilies. Chill. Before serving, stir in fruit. Sprinkle with pepper and serve. *Makes 1 quart.*

Note: Can be prepared in advance. Serve as appetizer with toasted French bread. Also serve with grilled veal, poultry, or spicy sausages.

JALAPEÑO BLACK-EYED PEA DIP

½   cup butter
½   pound sharp Cheddar cheese, grated
3   16-ounce cans black-eyed peas
½   cup chopped onions

4-6 jalapeños, seeded and chopped
1   teaspoon jalapeño juice
1   clove garlic, minced
1   4-ounce can chopped green chilies

In the top of a double boiler, melt butter and cheese. In a food processor fitted with a metal blade, process remaining ingredients. Stir mixture into cheese. Serve hot with tortilla chips.

SPICY GRILLED SHRIMP

1½ cups salad oil
¾   cup soy sauce
¼   cup Worcestershire sauce
2   Tablespoons dry mustard
1½ teaspoons salt
⅓   cup fresh lemon juice

4   teaspoons black pepper
¼   cup vinegar
½   cup white wine
1½ Tablespoons chopped parsley
3   cloves garlic, crushed
2-3 pounds uncooked shrimp, peeled

In a large bowl, mix all ingredients except shrimp. Stir in shrimp. Marinate 4-6 hours. Before serving, grill shrimp 10 minutes or until tender. *Serves 4-6.*

MARINATED CHICKEN SKEWERS

⅓   cup bourbon
¼   cup soy sauce
¼   cup firmly packed brown sugar
1   large onion, cut into 16 pieces
3   Tablespoons Dijon mustard
1   teaspoon Worcestershire

4   chicken breast halves, skinned, boned and quartered
8   slices bacon, cut in half
3   bell peppers, cut into a total of 16 pieces
16 medium mushrooms

In a small glass bowl, combine the bourbon, soy, sugar, onion, mustard and Worchestershire. Marinate chicken overnight. Wrap one-half bacon strip around each chicken piece. On a skewer, thread bacon-wrapped chicken, pepper, onion and mushrooms. Repeat 3 times. Before serving, grill skewers 20 minutes, turning once. *Serves 4.*

POPPY SEED CHEESE BREAD

2 packages active dry yeast	2 eggs, lightly beaten
1½ cups warm water	2 cups grated sharp cheese
2 Tablespoons sugar	⅛ cup poppy seeds (or caraway seed)
2¼ teaspoons salt	melted butter
6¼ -6½ cups flour	

In a large bowl, sprinkle yeast over water. Stir in sugar and salt until dissolved. Beat in 2 cups flour, eggs, cheese and poppy seeds. Work in 4 more cups of flour to make a soft dough, using hands if necessary. Turn out dough onto floured surface. Cover with bowl and let rest 10 minutes. Into dough knead enough remaining flour in small amounts to make it smooth and elastic with small blisters on the surface, about 8 minutes. Place dough in a large greased bowl. Cover and let rise in warm place (80-85°) until double in size, about 1½ hours. Punch down dough with your fist. Cover and let rise again until almost double in size. Grease two 8½ x 4½ x 2½-inch loaf pans. Punch dough down and turn out onto floured surface. Divide into 4 equal parts. With hands, roll each part into ropes 13 inches long. Twist 2 ropes together. Tuck ends under and put into pan. Repeat with remaining dough. Cover and let rise until almost double in size. Preheat oven to 350°. Brush tops of loaves with butter. Bake 35 minutes until brown and hollow sounding. Remove from pan. Brush with butter and cool on racks.

Note: Can be prepared and frozen.

GRAPE ICE CREAM

3 cups sugar	4 cups half-and-half cream
1 quart grape juice	
juice of 6 lemons	

In a large bowl, mix all ingredients. Freeze in ice cream freezer according to freezer instructions. *Serves 12-16.*

HONEY COOKIES

¾ cup butter, melted	2¼ cups flour
1 cup sugar	2 teaspoons baking soda
1 egg	½ teaspoon nutmeg
¼ cup honey	additional sugar

Preheat oven to 350°. In large bowl, mix butter and sugar. Blend in egg, honey and dry ingredients. Chill briefly if necessary to make dough easier to handle. Roll into small balls and coat with sugar. Bake on ungreased cookie sheets 8-10 minutes. *Makes 5 dozen.*

PRALINE ICE CREAM

4 eggs, separated	½ teaspoon salt
2 14-ounce cans sweetened condensed milk	2½ cups milk
	5 pralines, coarsely crumbled
1 quart half-and-half cream	2 Heath candy bars, coarsely crumbled
⅔ cup maple syrup	
1 teaspoon maple flavoring	

In large bowl, mix yolks, condensed milk, cream, syrup, flavoring, salt and milk. In separate bowl, beat whites until stiff. Fold whites into milk mixture. Freeze in ice cream freezer according to freezer instructions for 10 minutes. Stop machine. Fold candies into ice cream mixture and finish freezing. *Serves 10.*

LEMON SHERBET

3 cups milk or skim milk	⅔ cup fresh lemon juice
1 scant cup sugar	grated zest of 2 lemons

In a large bowl, mix all ingredients. Freeze in ice cream freezer according to freezer instructions. *Serves 4.*

HOLIDAY BRUNCH

Sausage Filled Crêpes With
Dill Sauce

French Custard Toast

Scrambled Eggs Magda

Cranberry Banana Bread

Hot Butter Muffins

Lemon Puff Coffee Cake

Orange Sticky Buns

Fresh Fruit With Jamaica
Sauce

Mimosas

Bloody Marys

ORANGE STICKY BUNS

Buns

¾ cup sugar	3½ cups flour
2 Tablespoons grated orange rind	2 Tablespoons butter, melted
1 envelope active dry yeast	
¼ cup very warm water	
¼ cup sugar	*Glaze*
1 teaspoon salt	¾ cup sugar
2 eggs	½ cup sour cream
½ cup sour cream	2 Tablespoons fresh orange juice
6 Tablespoons butter, melted	½ cup butter

To prepare buns: In a small bowl, mix sugar and rind and set aside. In a large bowl, dissolve yeast in water. Beat in sugar, salt, eggs, sour cream and butter. Gradually add 2 cups flour, beating until dough forms. Transfer to a floured surface. Into dough knead enough remaining flour in small amounts to make it smooth and elastic with small blisters on surface. Place dough in a large greased bowl. Cover and let rise in warm place (80-85°) until double in size, about 2 hours. Preheat oven to 350°. Punch dough down and turn out onto floured surface. Knead 15 times. Divide into 2 equal parts. Roll each part into a 12 inch circle. Brush circles with remaining butter. Sprinkle with orange-sugar mixture. Cut each circle into 12 pie-shape wedges. Starting at wide end, roll up wedges. Place point side down in greased 9x13-inch pan. Cover and let rise in warm place until almost double in size, about 1 hour. Bake uncovered 20 minutes or until golden brown. Glaze while still warm. *Makes 2 dozen.*

To prepare glaze: In a medium saucepan, mix all ingredients. Boil 3 minutes, stirring constantly. Spoon over hot rolls.

FRENCH CUSTARD TOAST

12 (1½-inches thick) slices day-old French bread	1½ Tablespoons lemon peel (optional)
4 eggs	1 teaspoon vanilla
4 cups evaporated or whole milk	½ teaspoon salt
	1 Tablespoon sugar
⅓ cup sugar	2 teaspoons cinnamon

Evenly divide bread slices between 2 greased 9x13-inch glass baking dishes. Set aside. In large bowl, whisk eggs, milk, sugar, peel, vanilla and salt. Pour evenly over bread. Let soak 5 minutes. Turn bread over. Cover and chill 12 hours. Before serving, preheat oven to 325°. In small bowl, mix sugar and cinnamon. Sprinkle evenly over bread. Bake uncovered 30-45 minutes. Serve immediately with powdered sugar, fresh fruit slices or maple syrup. *Serves 6.*

HOT BUTTER MUFFINS

⅓ cup butter, softened	¼ teaspoon nutmeg
½ cup sugar	½ cup milk
1 egg	½ cup sugar
1½ cups flour	1 teaspoon cinnamon
1½ teaspoons baking powder	½ cup butter, melted and cooled
½ teaspoon salt	

Preheat oven to 350°. In a large bowl, cream butter and sugar. Beat in egg. In small bowl, combine flour, baking powder, salt and nutmeg. Add alternately dry ingredients and milk to butter mixture. Fill greased mini-muffin tins ½ full and bake 15-20 minutes. While baking, in small bowl mix remaining sugar and cinnamon. When finished baking, remove muffins from pan. Roll first in butter, then in sugar mixture. Serve hot. *Makes 2 dozen.*

SCRAMBLED EGGS MAGDA

8	eggs	2	teaspoons chopped
	salt and pepper		mixed tarragon,
6	Tablespoons butter		chervil, and chives
¾	cup grated Gruyère	2	teaspoons Dijon
	cheese		mustard
		6	croustades

In large bowl, beat eggs, salt and pepper to taste until frothy. Set aside. In a heavy pan, melt butter. Add eggs and stir constantly until mixture begins to thicken. Stir in cheese until it melts. Remove from heat. Mix in herbs and mustard. Fill croustades. Serve immediately. *Serves 4-6.*

CRANBERRY BANANA BREAD

1	cup butter, softened	1	teaspoon salt
2	cups sugar	2	teaspoons baking soda
2	teaspoons vanilla	2	teaspoons baking
1	Tablespoon lemon juice		powder
4	eggs	1	cup sour cream
5	very ripe bananas (4	1-2	cups fresh cranberries
	mashed, 1 chopped)	½	cup chopped walnuts
3½	cups presifted flour		(optional)

Preheat oven to 350°. In a large bowl, cream butter and sugar. Beat in vanilla, lemon juice and eggs. Stir in mashed bananas. Combine flour, salt, soda and baking powder. Stir into banana mixture. Mix in sour cream, chopped banana, berries and nuts. Pour into 2 greased loaf pans. Bake 1 hour, 10-15 minutes. Cool in pans 20 minutes; turn out onto racks and cool completely. *Makes 2 loaves.*

Note: Can be frozen. Can substitute blueberries or raspberries for the cranberries. If very juicy, dust with flour before adding to batter.

LEMON PUFF COFFEE CAKE

Cake		Icing	
1	cup water	3	Tablespoons milk
½	cup butter	1	Tablespoon butter,
1	teaspoon sugar		melted
½	teaspoon salt	½	teaspoon vanilla
1	cup flour	½	teaspoon lemon juice
4	eggs	½	teaspoon almond
2	Tablespoons grated		extract
	lemon peel or 1	1-1½	cups powdered
	teaspoon lemon extract		sugar
¼	cup sliced almonds,		
	toasted		

To prepare cake: Preheat oven to 400°. In a saucepan, mix water, butter, sugar and salt. Bring to a boil. Add flour all at once. Beat with a wooden spoon until mixture forms a ball. Remove from heat and let cool 2 minutes. Transfer dough to a food processor. Add eggs one at a time, processing until egg is fully incorporated. Add lemon. Using a jelly roll pan, spread dough into two 3x15-inch strips. Bake 35 minutes, until puffed and golden. Decoratively drizzle icing over strips. Sprinkle with almonds and serve. *Makes two 3x15-inch cakes.*

To prepare icing: In a small saucepan, heat milk, butter, vanilla, juice and extract. Stir in 1 cup sugar; then add enough remaining sugar until icing reaches drizzling consistency. Drizzle over cakes. Icing will harden slightly.

OUTDOORS

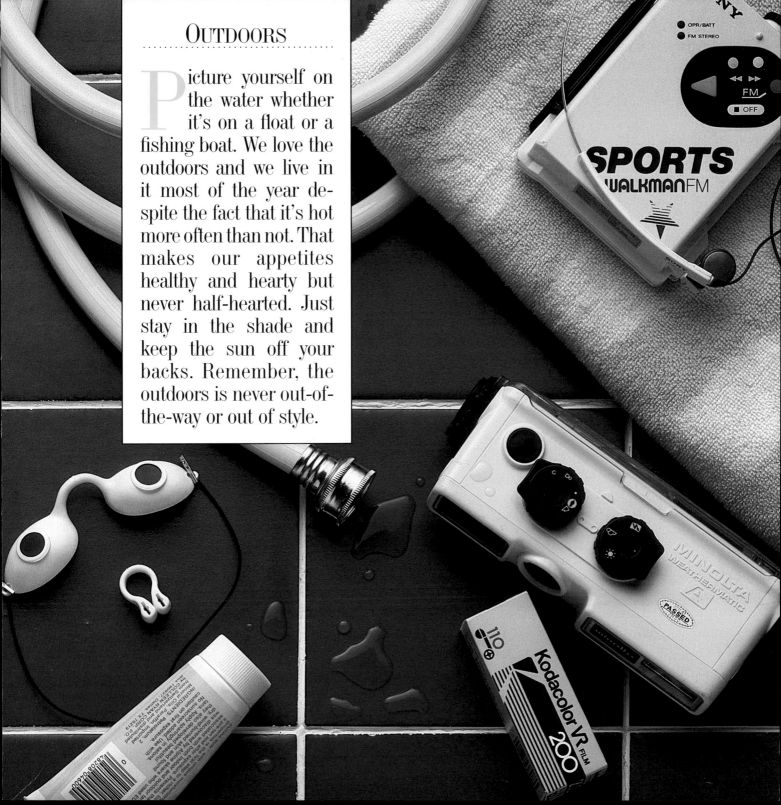

OUTDOORS

Picture yourself on the water whether it's on a float or a fishing boat. We love the outdoors and we live in it most of the year despite the fact that it's hot more often than not. That makes our appetites healthy and hearty but never half-hearted. Just stay in the shade and keep the sun off your backs. Remember, the outdoors is never out-of-the-way or out of style.

When it's time for a time-out in the great outdoors, Dallasites don't usually hang out indoors. We head for the Texas hills or coast, plains or piney woods to stretch our limbs and unwind our minds. And although it's camera country, we take part in the fun rather than just take pictures.

We can hunt, fish, swim or scuba on this huge Texas spread. Not only is there space enough for our natives, the deer, dove, duck, goose, quail, pheasant and turkey but there's also spare room for the rest of us who've migrated here. And in fresh water or salt, such a variety can be caught (crappie, catfish, sailfish, swordfish, blue marlin or black fin tuna) that gone fishin' doesn't just mean gone wishin'. Our trophies are usually served at dinner.

If you're a beachcomber with no beach, pool your resources with friends for a "Seafood Pool Party". When it's 90° a pool, even if it's plastic, whets the appetite, but won't dampen the feast. Sizzle the bacon over the grill and it will lend a delicate smoked flavor to fish. We tried this with Chama Trout (any lake or brookie will do), and we couldn't stop nibbling all night. Angel Hair Pasta is perfect bait for the lounge-chair loafer. He may complain about moving a muscle but this crab with noodles will get rid of his grumbles.

The spoils of hunting certainly won't spoil the appetite especially when a "Game Dinner" doesn't taste too gamey, just plain good. Your guests will want pointers on how to marinate this Saddleback Ranch Duck. There's no limit to the compliments you'll receive. The call of the Wild Mushroom Soup isn't strong, just creamy and smooth. Strawberry red is a safe color in the woods for our Fruit Trifle, especially if the whipped cream camouflages the macaroons. Whether picnic or potluck, classic or casual, try out these outstanding menus in the great outdoors.

OUTDOORS

SEAFOOD POOL PARTY

CURRY DIP WITH
FRESH CRUDITÉS
p. 66

COLD SHRIMP AND CHEESE TORTE
p. 67

ANGEL HAIR PASTA WITH CRAB
p. 67

TOMATOES STUFFED WITH
ARTICHOKE HEARTS IN
DILL SAUCE
p. 66

GRILLED CHAMA TROUT
p. 67

SPINACH AND MUSHROOM
FLORENTINE
p. 66

RASPBERRY ORANGE SUNDAES
p. 67

WINE COOLERS

GAME DINNER

QUAIL NACHOS
p. 70

CRAB AND ROASTED PEPPERS
p. 122

WILD MUSHROOM SOUP
p. 126

QUAIL SUPREME
p. 70

GRILLED VENISON TOURNEDOS
p. 70

SADDLEBACK RANCH GRILLED DUCK
p. 70

RASPBERRY GAME SAUCE
p. 71

CUMBERLAND SAUCE
p. 71

NUTTED WILD RICE
p. 182

CARAMEL AND NUT TARTLETS
p. 71

FRESH FRUIT TRIFLE
p. 193

Seafood Pool Party

Curry Dip With
Fresh Crudités

Cold Shrimp And Cheese
Torte

Angel Hair Pasta With Crab

Tomatoes Stuffed With
Artichoke Hearts In
Dill Sauce

Grilled Chama Trout

Spinach Mushroom Florentine

Raspberry Orange Sundae

Wine Coolers

CURRY DIP WITH FRESH CRUDITÉS

1	cup mayonnaise	½	teaspoon curry powder
2	teaspoons tarragon vinegar	2	teaspoons chili sauce
dash of pepper		2	teaspoons snipped fresh chives
½	teaspoon salt	2	Tablespoons grated onion
⅛	teaspoon dried thyme		

Mix all ingredients in a small bowl. Cover and chill. Serve with fresh vegetables.
Makes 1¼ cups.

SPINACH AND MUSHROOM FLORENTINE

3-4	cups fresh spinach, rinsed and trimmed	½	pound mushrooms, sliced
¼	cup chopped green onion		garlic salt
4	Tablespoons unsalted butter	1½	cups grated Swiss cheese

Preheat oven to 350°. Spread spinach in a 9x11-inch glass baking dish. In a medium skillet, sauté onion in butter. Add mushrooms and continue to sauté 2-3 minutes. Place sautéed mushrooms and onions over spinach. Season to taste with garlic salt. Top with cheese and bake for 15-20 minutes. *Serves 6.*

Note: Artichoke hearts can be nestled in spinach layer.

Wine Selection: Pheasant Ridge Sauvignon Blanc

TOMATOES STUFFED WITH ARTICHOKE HEARTS IN DILL SAUCE

6	large, ripe tomatoes		Dressing
salt and pepper		½	cup mayonnaise
fresh chopped dill		½	cup sour cream
12	artichoke hearts, coarsely chopped		juice of ½ lemon
¼	cup chopped green onion tops	1	teaspoon curry powder
		2	dill sprigs, chopped

Drop tomatoes in boiling water for 1 minute. Remove and peel skin. Cut top off of tomatoes and scoop out pulp. Season tomatoes inside and out with salt, pepper and dill. Combine artichoke hearts and green onion. Spoon artichoke mixture into tomato shells. Chill. To serve, spoon dressing over tomatoes and sprinkle with chopped dill. *Serves 6.*

To prepare dressing: In a small bowl, mix all ingredients and chill until ready to serve.

Note: For a variation, add cooked shrimp or chopped avocado to artichoke mixture. Cooked bacon can be crumbled over top.

Grilled Chama Trout

2   pounds fish fillets   1   onion, thinly sliced
    (preferably trout)   10   sprigs fresh cilantro
12 Tablespoons butter   6   slices raw bacon
seasoned salt and pepper   ½   lemon

Using a grill with a lid, let coals cook down to medium hot (30-45 minutes). Place butter in a large iron skillet. Melt butter and cook until lightly browned, about 10 minutes. Lay fish in pan and season to taste with salt and pepper. Add onion and cilantro. Lay raw bacon directly on grill around pan to create smoke. Cook fish for 10-12 minutes with grill covered, basting occasionally with butter sauce from pan (do not overcook). Squeeze lemon over fish and serve with butter sauce. Discard bacon. *Serves 4.*

Cold Shrimp And Cheese Torte

2   8-ounce packages   1   green pepper, chopped
    cream cheese, softened   3   tomatoes, chopped
2   cups chopped, cooked   6   green onions (green
    shrimp or crabmeat   and white parts),
12 ounces red cocktail   chopped
    sauce   crackers
10 ounces grated
    Mozzarella cheese

On a platter, layer cream cheese, shrimp, cocktail sauce and cheese. Combine green pepper, tomatoes and green onions. Sprinkle over top of torte. Chill. Serve with crackers. *Serves 12-15. Not pictured.*

Angel Hair Pasta With Crab

6   Tablespoons butter   ½   pound fresh lump
⅓   cup sliced green onion   crabmeat
    (green and white parts)   12   ounces angel hair
¼   cup finely chopped   pasta
    white onion   ½   cup grated Parmesan
1   clove garlic, minced   cheese
1   cup whipping cream

In a medium skillet, melt butter and sauté garlic and onions. Add whipping cream and boil until slightly thickened. Add crabmeat . In a large pot cook pasta in boiling salted water to al dente stage. Drain pasta and transfer to serving dish. Pour crab sauce over pasta. Add Parmesan cheese and toss thoroughly. Serve immediately. *Serves 6 as a first course, 4 as a main course.*

Raspberry Orange Sundaes

1   10-ounce package   2   Tablespoons fresh
    frozen raspberries,   orange juice
    thawed   1   quart vanilla ice cream
6   Tablespoons orange
    marmalade

In food processor fitted with metal blade or blender, process raspberries until liquified. Strain through sieve to remove seeds and set aside. In a small saucepan, melt marmalade over low heat. Add orange juice and blend. Scoop ice cream into individual dishes and top half of scoop with raspberry sauce and the remaining half with warm orange sauce. *Serves 10.*

GAME DINNER

QUAIL NACHOS

CRAB AND ROASTED PEPPERS

WILD MUSHROOM SOUP

QUAIL SUPREME

GRILLED VENISON TOURNEDOS

SADDLEBACK RANCH GRILLED DUCK

RASPBERRY GAME SAUCE

CUMBERLAND SAUCE

FRESH STEAMED ASPARAGUS

NUTTED WILD RICE

CARAMEL AND NUT TARTLETS

FRESH FRUIT TRIFLE

WINE

QUAIL NACHOS

6   quail, cleaned
unsalted butter, melted
1   red bell pepper, cut into
    3-inch slivers
grated Monterey Jack
    cheese
grated Colby cheese
tostado chips
jalapeños (optional)

To prepare quail: In a large skillet, brown quail in butter. Add red bell pepper, cover skillet and cook over low heat until tender. Remove quail from skillet and separate meat from bones. Keep quail warm.

To prepare nachos: Place small portion of meat and a red pepper sliver on each tostado chip. Sprinkle with cheeses, top with jalapeños and broil until cheese melts. Serve immediately. *Serves 10-12.*

QUAIL SUPREME

12 Quail
4-6 Tablespoons butter
½   cup flour
1   cup water
1   bay leaf
¼   cup celery
1   Tablespoon parsley
1   teaspoon salt
¼   teaspoon pepper
12 ounces beef broth
½   cup sherry
½   cup sour cream
1   chopped onion

Brown quail in butter in a large skillet. Remove and keep warm. Spread flour on shallow pan and brown in 350° oven. Add flour to skillet and blend over medium heat adding more butter if necessary. Add water, bay leaf, celery, parsley, salt, pepper, onion and beef broth. Add birds and simmer for 1 hour. When ready to serve, remove birds and stir in sherry. Cook for 5 additional minutes. Stir in sour cream. Serve over birds with wild rice or noodles. *Makes 6 servings.*

SADDLEBACK RANCH GRILLED DUCK

6-8 wild ducks, well
    cleaned
6   ounces orange juice
    concentrate, defrosted
1   cup brown sugar
½   cup orange marmalade
2   or more cups soy sauce

Marinate ducks in deep pot at least 4 hours in refrigerator. Remove from marinade. Cook over hottest charcoal fire until medium-rare (about 16 minutes). If larger domestic duck is substituted allow 1 duck for 2 persons.

Note: Build fire with all of a 10-pound bag of charcoal. When fire is burning at its hottest point, add 4 pieces of presoaked wood chips. Sear breast side of ducks, then turn so that back side is over the fire. Cover charcoal grill with lid, closing all air vents and cook until ducks are medium-rare. Ducks will be heavily charred on the outside.

GRILLED VENISON TOURNEDOS

1   cup water
1   bay leaf, crumbled
6   whole cloves
1   small onion, sliced
½   teaspoon thyme
1   cup dry red wine
2   Tablespoons oil
salt and pepper
3-4 venison tenderloins, 1¼
    -1½ pounds each

In a small saucepan, heat water to boiling point. Place bay leaf, cloves, onion and thyme in a nonmetal flat dish and pour heated water over them. Cool, add wine and oil and stir to mix. Add meat to dish and more water to cover. Cover dish and refrigerate two hours. Allow coals on grill to cook down to medium hot. Remove meat from marinade and dry with paper towels. Grill for 7 minutes on each side or until medium rare. Remove from grill and slice slightly on the diagonal about ¾-inch thick to form tournedos. *Serves 12-14.*

Note: Size of tenderloins may vary due to type of deer. Backstrap may also be used.

RASPBERRY GAME SAUCE

4	10-ounce packages frozen raspberries	6	Tablespoons sugar
1	cup cold water	1-2	scant Tablespoons lemon juice
3	Tablespoons arrowroot		

Defrost berries and purée in food processor. Strain to remove seeds and reserve purée. In a medium saucepan, combine water, arrowroot and sugar. Cook over low heat until clear and thickened. Add berry purée. Cook 5 minutes longer. Remove from heat and add lemon juice. Serve warm. *Makes 4 cups.*

CUMBERLAND SAUCE

½	orange	¼	teaspoon ground ginger
½	lemon		dash of cayenne pepper
½	cup water	½	cup white raisins
4	Tablespoons red currant jelly	½	cup port wine
½	cup port wine	½	cup blanched slivered almonds
1	teaspoon dry mustard		
1	Tablespoon light brown sugar		

With a zester, remove strips of zest from lemon and orange halves. Juice fruit and set aside. Put zest and water in a small saucepan and bring to a boil. Drain, discarding water and reserving zest. Melt jelly over low heat. Add ½ cup wine, orange and lemon zest and juice. Mix dry mustard, brown sugar and ginger and add to jelly mixture along with cayenne pepper. Bring sauce to boil. Place over simmering water to keep warm. In a small saucepan, plump raisins in ½ cup boiling wine for two minutes. Add raisins and port with almonds to sauce and serve warm. *Makes 2 cups sauce.*

CARAMEL AND NUT TARTLETS

Pastry		Filling	
1½	cups flour	1¼	cups sugar
3	Tablespoons sugar	5½	Tablespoons water
¼	teaspoon salt	⅛	teaspoon cream of tartar
½	cup butter, chilled	⅔	cup whipping cream
¼	cup vegetable shortening, chilled	¾	cup chopped walnuts or pecans
1	egg, beaten with 1 Tablespoon water	7	Tablespoons butter, cut into small pieces

To prepare pastry: In food processor fitted with metal blade, combine flour, sugar and salt. Add butter and shortening and process until mixture resembles coarse meal. With machine running, add egg mixture a little at a time until dough begins to hold together. Shape dough into ball. Wrap in plastic wrap and refrigerate at least 30 minutes.

Preheat oven to 400°. On a lightly floured surface, roll dough out to ⅛ inch thickness. Using a 3-inch cookie cutter, cut dough into 3-inch circles and press into buttered 2-inch tartlet pans. Place a small piece of foil in each tartlet shell and weight with beans or pie weights. Bake 15 minutes. Remove foil and weights and bake until lightly golden, about 5 minutes. Cool on racks and remove from pans.

To prepare filling: Combine sugar, water and cream of tartar, swirling to blend (do not stir). Cook over high heat without stirring until mixture reaches 334° on candy thermometer. While heating, wash down any sugar crystals clinging to the side of the pan with a brush dipped in cold water. Do not overcook. Remove from heat and let stand 15 seconds. Add cream and swirl gently until foam subsides, do not stir. Gently mix in nuts. Place pieces of butter on top of mixture and let melt completely. Stir until just blended. Return caramel to low heat and cook, stirring constantly for 5 to 6 minutes. Fill tartlet shells. *Makes 36 tartlets.*

UNDER THE STARS

Junior
Assembly
'58

CRISTAL
LOUIS
ROEDERER

CHAMPAGNE

LOUIS ROEDERER

UNDER THE STARS

A beautiful evening "Under The Stars" can be as perfect as a pearl, as exquisite as a gardenia. Be as inventive as Galileo! Place mirrors under your candles for a heavenly glow or spread glitter on your table as moondrops. If you're stargazing on the water, be less formal. For decoration sand dollars require only a small investment. Even the sandman won't sleep this night!

On a clear night you can see forever. Certainly it's on those sapphire and stardusted evenings that a gathering of special friends is as magical as a midsummer night's dream.

You only need to reserve a small piece of sky for the occasion. At the pool, patio, penthouse, garden or anywhere you can put the bugs to bed early. And because the Dallas climate is temperate most months of the year, you and your guests can catch falling stars from dusk to dawn.

For a glittering stardate, design a menu that is as beautiful and elegant as the constellation you will dine under: that of Cygnus, the Swan. Don't limit your universe. Polish your table by the light of the silvery moon with heirlooms that will shine and treasures that will twinkle. Although your menu could be as infinite and varied as the Milky Way, our horoscope suggests "A Candlelight Dinner for Eight". Enchant your guests with an appetizer from out of this world. And for a bit of heaven, serve tender Veal Chops with Crème Fraîche. Your finest china, backlighted with linen and lace, sets not only the table but also the romantic mood.

If you're feeling landlocked, invite a few landlubbers on deck to try out their sea legs. Let the water be your oyster to celebrate a sunset, catch a fish or make a wish. No yachts required for our "Boating Party".

With the constellation Pisces overhead, it's easy to entertain nautically. A real sailor's delight is the Shrimp Bread, served sandwich style, or the Regatta Salad, a contender for America's most unusual cup of tasty ingredients. But the real catch of the day remains the Mocha Chocolate Cheesecake, dotted with chocolate curls and strawberries. Even Renoir never enjoyed such a boating party. Spin the compass in all directions for an evening of fine dining under the stars.

UNDER THE STARS

CANDLELIGHT DINNER FOR EIGHT

ASPARAGUS PROSCIUTTO ROLLS
p. 80

VEAL CHOPS WITH
CRÈME FRAÎCHE
p. 80

CARROT PURÉE
p. 80

BROWN RICE PILAF
WITH RAISINS
p. 81

RASPBERRY TART
p. 81

WINE

ON THE WATER

SHRIMP BREAD
p. 85

TOMATO TART
p. 85

REGATTA SALAD
p. 84

MIXED GREENS WITH TOASTED
WALNUTS AND BERRIES WITH
SHERRY VINAIGRETTE
p. 84

MOCHA CHOCOLATE CHEESECAKE
p. 85

78

CANDLELIGHT DINNER FOR EIGHT

ASPARAGUS PROSCIUTTO ROLLS

VEAL CHOPS WITH
CRÈME FRAÎCHE

CARROT PURÉE

BROWN RICE PILAF
WITH RAISINS

RASPBERRY TART

WINE

ESPRESSO

ASPARAGUS PROSCIUTTO ROLLS

24 pieces thinly sliced homemade-style white bread, crusts removed	8 ounces cream cheese, cut into 24 slices
½ cup stone ground mustard	12 thin slices prosciutto, halved
½ cup orange marmalade	6 Tablespoons unsalted butter, melted
24 medium spears fresh asparagus, trimmed	

Preheat oven to 350°. Flatten bread with a rolling pin and cover with a damp cloth. In a small bowl, mix mustard and marmalade; reserve. Blanch asparagus in boiling water for one minute. Spread mustard-marmalade mixture on one slice of bread (keep remaining bread covered with damp towel). Place an asparagus spear and a piece of cream cheese on one slice of prosciutto and roll prosciutto. Place prosciutto on bread and roll like a jellyroll. Place on a cookie sheet, seam side down. Repeat process with remaining slices of bread. Rolls can be refrigerated or frozen at this point. To bake, brush tops with butter and bake for 15 minutes or until golden brown. *Serves 12.*

CARROT PURÉE

1 pound carrots, peeled and coarsely chopped	3 Tablespoons sour cream
4 Tablespoons unsalted butter	salt and white pepper
¼ cup whipping cream	

In a medium saucepan, melt butter and sauté carrots over lowest heat for 20 to 25 minutes until tender. Transfer carrots to food processor fitted with metal blade; process until smooth. Add whipping cream and sour cream; process until blended. If purée is too thick, add more sour cream by teaspoons to attain desired consistency. Season to taste with salt and white pepper. Serve hot. *Serves 4.*

VEAL CHOPS WITH CRÈME FRAÎCHE

9 ounces mushrooms, sliced	Crème Fraîche
1 Tablespoon unsalted butter	1 cup sour cream
4 Tablespoons unsalted butter	1 cup whipping cream
1 Tablespoon oil	
8 veal chops	
1 cup grated Comte or Gruyère cheese	
1 Tablespoon Cognac	
1 cup Crème Fraîche	
¼ teaspoon salt	
¼ teaspoon pepper	

To prepare veal: In a large skillet over low heat, melt 1 Tablespoon butter and sauté mushrooms until brown. Remove mushrooms with a slotted spoon and set aside. Turn the heat to medium-high and sauté veal chops in 4 Tablespoons butter and oil until well browned, approximately 5 minutes on each side (cook veal chops in two batches, discarding the butter/oil mixture if it gets too dark). Remove chops to an ovenproof platter; top with cheese and keep warm. Deglaze the skillet with the Cognac. Add Crème Fraîche, mushrooms, ¼ teaspoon salt and ¼ teaspoon pepper; stir well. Pour sauce over chops and serve. *Serves 8.*

To prepare Crème Fraîche: Whisk sour cream and whipping cream together. Place in a covered glass jar and let stand at room temperature for 12 to 24 hours or until thickened. Refrigerate for at least 4 hours before using. Will keep in the refrigerator for three weeks.
Makes 2 cups.

Note: Veal scallops (2 pounds) can be substituted for veal chops. Cook scallops 1-1½ minutes on each side.

FRESH RASPBERRY TART

Crust	Pastry Cream
½ cup butter, room temperature	2 egg yolks, room temperature
2½ Tablespoons sugar	2½ Tablespoons sugar
½ cup finely chopped pecans	2 Tablespoons cornstarch
1 egg, beaten to blend	½ teaspoon vanilla
1 teaspoon almond extract	⅔ cup milk
1⅓ cups flour	6 Tablespoons butter, room temperature
	4 cups fresh raspberries
	1 cup red currant jelly
	1 Tablespoon brandy
	lightly sweetened whipped cream

To prepare crust: Butter a 10 or 11-inch tart pan with a removable bottom. In a large bowl, cream butter, vanilla and sugar. Mix in nuts. Blend in egg and almond extract. Stir in flour until completely incorporated. Press dough into prepared pan. Refrigerate 30 minutes. While shell is chilling, preheat oven to 350°. Bake shell for 20 minutes until golden brown. Cool to room temperature. Crust can be frozen in the pan after baking if well wrapped.

To prepare pastry cream: In a medium bowl, beat egg yolks, sugar and cornstarch until pale and thick. Heat milk in a small saucepan. Beat milk into yolk mixture until smooth. Return combined mixture to saucepan and whisk over medium heat until very thick. Return mixture to bowl and beat until cool. Beat in butter, one Tablespoon at a time until fully incorporated. Cover with plastic wrap touching the top surface to prevent a skin from forming. Refrigerate until well chilled or up to 2 days.

To assemble tart: Spread pastry cream evenly over bottom of crust. Starting from outside edge, arrange berries in concentric circles over pastry cream, placing berries as close together as possible. Refrigerate 30 minutes. In a small saucepan over low heat, melt red currant jelly, stirring occasionally. Remove from heat and add brandy. Gently spoon or brush glaze over berries, covering completely. Refrigerate at least 2 hours. Serve with lightly sweetened whipped cream. *Serves 12.*

BROWN RICE PILAF WITH NUTS AND RAISINS

4 Tablespoons unsalted butter (or 2 Tablespoons butter and 2 Tablespoons oil)	2 Tablespoons unsalted butter, melted	
¼ cup chopped onion	½ cup golden raisins	
1 cup brown rice	½ cup dry white wine	
2½ cups chicken stock or water	¾ cup almonds, toasted	
1 teaspoon salt	½ cup mint or coriander, chopped	
¼ teaspoon pepper	fresh mint or coriander for garnish	

In a medium saucepan, sauté the onions in 4 Tablespoons of butter until translucent. Add rice and cook over low heat until grains are coated with butter and have browned a little, about 3 minutes. Add stock or water, stir and season with salt and pepper. Bring to a boil. Cover and simmer for 45 minutes or until all the liquid is absorbed. Meanwhile, plump raisins in white wine. Remove rice from heat and toss in melted butter. Add almonds and raisins and chopped mint or coriander to rice and mix well. Turn into serving bowl and garnish with mint or coriander. *Serves 4.*

Wine Selection: Llano Estacado Chardonnay

On The Water

Shrimp Bread

Tomato Tart

Regatta Salad

Mixed Greens With Toasted
Walnuts And Berries With
Sherry Vinaigrette

Mocha Chocolate Cheesecake

MIXED GREENS WITH TOASTED WALNUTS & BERRIES WITH SHERRY VINAIGRETTE

Salad

1   cup walnut halves, toasted and skinned
2   Tablespoons butter, melted
1   small head red tip leaf lettuce
1   bunch watercress or lambs lettuce
1   head bibb lettuce
1   cup fresh blueberries or raspberries

Dressing

1   shallot or clove garlic, minced
1   teaspoon dry mustard
1   teaspoon salt
¼   teaspoon white pepper
¼   cup sherry wine vinegar
¼   cup walnut oil, warmed
½   cup safflower oil

To prepare salad: In a small skillet, sauté nuts in butter several minutes. Drain and set aside. In a large bowl, tear lettuces into bite-size pieces. Add watercress and toss well. Chill. Before serving, toss nuts with lettuce; mix in dressing. Garnish with berries. *Serves 6.*

To prepare dressing: In blender or food processor fitted with metal blade, mix all ingredients. Immediately pour over salad.

REGATTA SALAD

Salad

1   pound lean chicken, cooked and diced
6   ounces cooked sweet corn
4   ounces mushrooms, sliced
2   cups cooked rice
2-3 shallots, chopped
2   Tablespoons chopped chives
2   Tablespoons chopped parsley
2   medium peaches, sliced
1   ripe avocado, peeled, pitted and sliced
juice of 1 lemon

Dressing

¾   cup mayonnaise
2   ounces whipping cream, whipped until thick
2   Tablespoons lemon juice
1-2 teaspoons curry powder
1   teaspoon salt
½   teaspoon black pepper
½   teaspoon cayenne

To prepare salad: In a large bowl, combine chicken, corn, mushrooms, rice, shallots, chives and parsley. Fold in dressing. Chill tightly covered, tossing occasionally. To serve, coat peaches and avocado with lemon juice; toss into salad. *Serves 6.*

To prepare dressing: In a small bowl, whisk mayonnaise and lemon juice. Mix in remaining ingredients. Can be prepared in advance.

SHRIMP BREAD

2	8-10 inch baguettes
1	clove garlic, peeled
½	cup parsley
½	cup unsalted butter, softened

	salt and pepper
2	teaspoons white wine
1	pound medium shrimp, peeled, deveined, raw
1	Tablespoon white wine

Preheat oven to 400°. To form the shell, slice top off bread, forming a lid. Hollow out loaf, leaving ½-inch rim all around. Set aside. In food processor, grind hollowed out bread pieces into crumbs; set aside. In processor, mince garlic and parsley. Add butter, salt, pepper and 2 teaspoons wine. Process until smooth. Spread thin layer of butter on inside of bread shell. Layer ¼ of shrimp inside shell. Sprinkle with salt and pepper. Top with thin layer of butter followed by a generous layer of crumbs. Repeat butter, shrimp and crumb layers. Dot top layer of crumbs with butter. Sprinkle with ½ Tablespoon wine. Repeat process with second baguette. Place lids on top; wrap loaves in foil. Can be frozen at this point. Thaw before baking. Bake 30 minutes. Slice and serve at once. *Serves 6-8.*

MOCHA CHOCOLATE CHEESECAKE

2	cups crushed chocolate wafers
4	Tablespoons butter, melted
3	8-ounce packages cream cheese, softened
1	cup sugar

3	eggs
1	Tablespoon instant coffee
⅓	cup Amaretto
2	cups sour cream
1	6-ounce package chocolate chips

Preheat oven to 350°. In a medium bowl, mix wafers and butter; press into a greased 9-inch springform pan. In a large bowl, beat cream cheese and sugar. Blend in eggs one at a time. Stir in coffee, Amaretto and sour cream. Beat 2 minutes at medium speed. Stir in chips. Pour into pan. Bake 50-60 minutes. *Serves 8-12.*

Wine Selection: Light Chardonnay or Sauvignon Blanc

TOMATO TART

1	9-inch baked pie crust
1	Tablespoon grated Parmesan cheese
5	medium-large tomatoes, sliced
	salt and pepper
½	teaspoon oregano
1	cup chopped green onions
1	cup mayonnaise
2	cups grated sharp Cheddar cheese

½	cup grated Parmesan cheese
2	small tomatoes, very thinly sliced

Preheat oven to 400°. When heated, reduce to 325°. Drain sliced tomatoes on paper towelling for 15 minutes. Sprinkle bottom of crust with 1 Tablespoon Parmesan. Cover cheese with 2 layers of tomatoes, using half of the slices. Sprinkle with salt and pepper, ¼ teaspoon oregano and ½ cup onions. Repeat layers. In a small bowl, combine mayonnaise and Cheddar cheese and spread over layers. Top with Parmesan. Decoratively arrange remaining tomato slices on top of tart. Bake 50 minutes. Tomatoes may be juicy but this is normal. Serve at room temperature. *Serves 6-8.*

Note: Can be prepared in advance and chilled. Bring to room temperature.

TIME CAPSULE

TIME CAPSULE

Fill your Time Capsule with some souvenirs of years shared. For any reunion, recreate the music, mood and dress of the times (and any stories you care to remember). If you're celebrating a special birthday; posters, slides and home movies may provide a new perspective on an old friend. Give a sentimental gift, like a framed photo, but stay away from the overused theme of black. We suggest purple, a color signifying royalty and loyalty.

If you're feeling antique or obsolete, bring back the days of "doo-wah" and Dick Clark. Whether you were neat, nerd or nameless, our Time Capsule defies gray hair and gravity around the waistline.

Invite Annette and Elvis, Fabian and Frankie to twist and shout, jitter and jerk the night away. And don't forget your annual and autographs, forty-fives and photographs. Top honors go to the valedictorian of teen trivia! Don't let your school "Reunion" be limited to memories of mystery meat and keep the mashed potato where it belongs (on the dance floor). Even if you're serving cafeteria style, this celebration can be as classic as Coca-Cola.

In French, we never accented hors d'oeuvres like Asparagus Dijonnaise and no lunch line presented anything similar to Marinated Beef Tenderloin without the ghost of gravies past. If only that little Italian restaurant your prom date recommended had served Seafood Fettucine Primavera instead of pizza with anchovies, you might still have his ring. Fortunately, there's no legal age limit on Cassata, a wonderfully rich, chocolate brandy dessert. These days your face will break out only with a smile!

No mourning or mid-life crisis for our "Fortieth Birthday". Leave wrinkles, pounds and pills over the hill and celebrate feeling fabulous, even if your figure isn't. If you organize a surprise for a good friend, serve Salmon Cornucopia Canapés, and she'll forgive you before the evening is over. Our recipe for Plum Sauce for Lamb is easy and elegant and we promise it won't age the hostess. And the Creamy Caramel Cake is a dessert which no one can deny. It's your party and you can cry if you want to but our Time Capsule should help you not only with smooth take-offs but also soft landings.

TIME CAPSULE

REUNION BUFFET

ASPARAGUS DIJONAISSE
p. 94

CREAMY CHICKEN LIVER PÂTÉ
p. 122

MARINATED BEEF TENDERLOIN
WITH GREEN PEPPERCORN
BUTTER
p. 94

HERB BUTTER
p. 95

SEAFOOD FETTUCINE PRIMAVERA
p. 95

TOMATOES IN DILL SAUCE
p. 94

GREEN SALAD WITH BLEU
CHEESE VINAIGRETTE
p. 132

CASSATA
p. 95

CUSTARDS GRAND MARNIER
p. 193

FORTIETH BIRTHDAY

SALMON CORNUCOPIA CANAPÉS
p. 98

CHOU-FLEUR SOUP
p. 98

FOUR LETTUCE SALAD WITH
MUSTARD VINAIGRETTE
p. 98

PLUM SAUCE FOR LAMB
p. 99

SOUBISE
p. 99

JULIENNED ZUCCHINI IN
GARLIC BUTTER
p. 175

CREAMY CARAMEL CAKE
p. 99

Reunion Buffet

Asparagus Dijonaisse

Creamy Chicken Liver Pâté

Marinated Beef Tenderloin

Green Peppercorn Butter

Herb Butter

Seafood Fettucine Primavera

Tomatoes In Dill Sauce

Green Salad With Bleu
Cheese Vinaigrette

Cassata

Custards Grand Marnier

ASPARAGUS DIJONNAISE

1	well shaped artichoke	2	Tablespoons Dijon
2-3	pounds fresh		mustard (or to taste)
	asparagus, trimmed	1	teaspoon lemon juice
1	cup mayonnaise		

Trim artichoke points and stem; steam for 45 minutes over medium-high heat. Cool. Remove top and inner leaves to make a bowl shape. Set aside. Steam asparagus until it turns bright green and somewhat soft. Rinse in cold water to stop cooking process. Mix remaining ingredients in small bowl; pour into cooled artichoke. Arrange asparagus around artichoke for dipping into mayonnaise. *Serves 4.*

Note: Can be prepared in advance but do not spoon mayonnaise into artichoke until immediately prior to serving.

TOMATOES IN DILL SAUCE

4	medium tomatoes, thickly sliced	1	cup sour cream
1	teaspoon salt	1	teaspoon dried dill weed
½	teaspoon pepper	½-¾	cup fresh buttered bread crumbs
6	green onions, chopped		

Preheat oven to 400°. In greased casserole dish, place one-half of tomatoes; sprinkle with half the salt, pepper and chopped onions. Repeat layers. Cover with sour cream; sprinkle with dill and crumbs. Bake 25 minutes or until brown. *Serves 6-8.*

MARINATED BEEF TENDERLOIN WITH GREEN PEPPERCORN BUTTER

Beef

2	cups port wine
½	cup oil
1	small onion, chopped or 5 green onions, chopped
1-2	cloves garlic, crushed and minced
	salt and pepper
2-4	bay leaves (or to taste)
5-6	pounds beef tenderloin

Green Peppercorn Butter

¾	cup butter
3	Tablespoons drained green peppercorns
1	Tablespoon chopped parsley
1	teaspoon Dijon mustard
	salt to taste

To prepare beef: In a medium-size bowl, mix well all ingredients except tenderloin. Pour over tenderloin and marinate 6-12 hours. Before serving, preheat oven to 425°. Remove tenderloin from marinade; pat dry. Place in a low roasting pan on rack. Bake uncovered 45-50 minutes or until meat thermometer reaches 150° for medium rare. Serve with Green Peppercorn Butter or Herb Butter. *Serves 10.*

To prepare butter: In food processor, purée all ingredients. Form into 1-inch thick log; roll in waxed paper and chill. To serve, cut butter into 1-inch slices, then allow to soften at room temperature. *Makes ¾ cup.*

Note: For a variation, remove meat from marinade, pat dry, roll in cracked pepper, lightly pressing the pepper into meat's surface. Bake.

HERB BUTTER

1	cup butter, room temperature
4	cloves garlic
2	green onions, green parts only
1	Tablespoon parsley, chopped
1	teaspoon dried basil
1	teaspoon dried oregano

In a food processor fitted with a metal blade, drop garlic through feed tube with machine running to chop finely. Add onion tops and chop. Add remaining ingredients and process until will mixed. *Makes 1 cup.*

SEAFOOD FETTUCINI PRIMAVERA

3	Tablespoons butter, melted
3	Tablespoons oil
½	pound mushrooms, sliced
2	carrots, julienned
1	cup broccoli flowerettes
2	cloves garlic, minced
1	pound bay scallops or shrimp or combination of each
1½	cups half-and-half cream
1	Tablespoon Dijon mustard
2	egg yolks, slightly beaten
¼	cup grated Parmesan cheese
8	ounces spinach fettucini, cooked

In a wok or large skillet, combine butter and oil; add mushrooms, carrots, broccoli and garlic. Stir-fry until crisp tender. Remove and set aside. Stir-fry seafood about 3-5 minutes; remove and set aside. Combine cream and mustard in skillet; simmer 3-5 minutes. Add a little of the hot cream to the yolks. Mix and return to the skillet. Stir in cheese. Add vegetables, seafood, pasta; toss well and serve. *Serves 4-6.*

CASSATA

Cake

1	pound cake
1	pound ricotta cheese
2	Tablespoons whipping cream
¼	cup sugar
4	Tablespoons orange-flavored liqueur
3	Tablespoons coarsely chopped dried figs
2	ounces semisweet chocolate, coarsely chopped

Icing

12	ounces semisweet chocolate, cut into small pieces
¾	cup strong black coffee
1	cup unsalted butter, cut into ½-inch pieces and well chilled

To prepare cake: trim top and sides from cake; discard. Slice lengthwise into 6 horizontal layers. Set aside. In a large bowl, beat ricotta until smooth. Add cream and sugar and beat until smooth. Fold in figs and chocolate. Center bottom slice of cake on a plate. Sprinkle with some of the liqueur; spread generously with ricotta mixture. Place another slice on top and repeat with liqueur and ricotta. Repeat until all slices are used, ending with plain top. Press down gently, making sure all slices are even. Chill until firm, about 2-3 hours, before frosting.

To prepare icing: In a small heavy saucepan, melt chocolate with coffee over low heat, stirring constantly until dissolved. Remove from heat; beat in butter, 1 piece at a time, with a small whisk until mixture is smooth. Chill to thicken to spreading consistency.

Frost cake. Cover loosely and chill at least 24 hours before serving. Slice cake thinly. *Serves 12.*

Wine Selection: Fall Creek Carnelian

Fortieth Birthday

Salmon Cornucopia Canapés

Chou-Fleur Soup

Four Lettuce Salad With
Mustard Vinaigrette

Plum Sauce For Lamb

Soubise

Julienned Zucchini In
Garlic Butter

Creamy Caramel Cake

SALMON CORNUCOPIA CANAPÉS

8 ounces cream cheese, softened	1 teaspoon Dijon mustard
½ cup butter, softened	½ teaspoon anchovy paste
2 Tablespoons minced onion	24 3-inch thin whole wheat fluted bread rounds
1 Tablespoon capers, drained	24 2½- inch pieces smoked salmon
1 Tablespoon paprika	Additional capers, well drained, for garnish
1½ teaspoons fresh lemon juice	

Beat until smooth all ingredients except bread, salmon and additional capers for garnish. Refrigerate overnight. When ready to serve, soften cream cheese mixture; spread on fluted bread rounds. Top each round with a cornucopia made of smoked salmon. Place additional capers at large end of cornucopia, to look as if they are spilling out. *Serves 12.*

Wine Selection: Champagne

MUSTARD VINAIGRETTE

Juice of ½ lemon	1 large clove garlic, crushed
1 egg yolk	salt and pepper
1½-2 Tablespoons red wine vinegar or tarragon vinegar	½ cup extra-virgin olive oil
2-3 Tablespoons Dijon mustard	½ cup peanut or other oil
2 shallots, minced	

Mix all ingredients with a wire whisk. Consistency should be like a thin mayonnaise. *Makes 1½ cups.*

Note: Suggested lettuce: Boston, red leaf, romaine and bibb.

CHOU-FLEUR SOUP

½ head cauliflower, cooked	1 Tablespoon cornstarch
1 medium potato, boiled and skinned	1 teaspoon seasoning salt
juice of ¼ lemon	1 cup milk
1 cup water	½ cup whipping cream
2 Tablespoons butter	4 teaspoons hot sauce
	4 Tablespoons grated Parmesan cheese

Purée first 4 ingredients in blender until smooth. Transfer mixture to saucepan; add butter and cook, stirring constantly, until thoroughly blended and butter is melted. Add cornstarch and salt; blend. Add milk, continuing to cook until edges boil; add cream, stirring constantly. Remove from heat. Stir in hot sauce. Pour into serving bowls; sprinkle with Parmesan cheese. May be doubled. *Serves 2.*

PLUM SAUCE FOR LAMB

½ cup plum jelly	½ cup red wine vinegar
1 Tablespoon dry mustard	2 heaping Tablespoons fresh chopped mint
½ cup brown sugar	1 leg of lamb, butterflied

In a saucepan, combine jelly, mustard, sugar and vinegar. Heat until jelly and sugar melt; simmer 5 minutes. Remove from heat and stir in mint. Grill lamb. (Baste with sauce the last 5-10 minutes of lamb grilling time. Don't baste too soon or sauce will char.) Serve sauce with lamb. *Serves 8.*

SOUBISE

½ cup rice	½ teaspoon pepper
4 quarts boiling water	½ cup whipping cream
2 teaspoons salt, divided	1 cup grated Swiss cheese
6 Tablespoons butter	chopped parsley
4 yellow onions, thinly sliced (about 6-7 cups)	

Preheat oven to 325°. Cook rice in rapidly boiling water with 1½ teaspoons salt for 5 minutes. Drain immediately. Put butter in casserole dish and heat in oven until foaming; stir in onions, coating well with the butter. Stir in rice, remaining salt and pepper. Cover; bake for 1 hour. Stir occasionally. Just before serving, stir in cream and cheese. Pour immediately into serving dish and sprinkle parsley on top. *Serves 4.*

CREAMY CARAMEL CAKE

Cake	Caramel Icing
¾ cup butter, softened	3 cups sugar
2 cups sugar	2 cups whipping cream
3 cups sifted cake flour	¼ cup butter
2 teaspoons baking powder	¼ cup light corn syrup
1 cup milk	1 Tablespoon vanilla
1 teaspoon vanilla	
5 egg whites, room temperature	

To prepare cake: Preheat oven to 350°. Cream butter, gradually add sugar, beating until light and fluffy . Combine flour and baking powder; add to creamed mixture alternately with milk, beginning and ending with flour mixture. Stir in vanilla. In a separate bowl, beat egg whites until stiff; fold into creamed mixture. Pour mixture into greased and floured 9-inch cake pans. Bake 25-30 minutes. Do not overcook. Cool in pans 10 minutes; remove from pans and cool completely. Frost and serve. *Serves 10.*

To prepare icing: Combine all ingredients except vanilla in a 3 or 4-quart heavy pot. Cook over medium heat, stirring often, until candy thermometer reaches 234° or soft ball stage. Remove from heat and cool approximately 5 minutes. Add vanilla. Icing hardens as it cools so spread immediately on cake, working quickly. If icing becomes too thick, thin with a little cream.

SWEET ENDINGS

SWEET ENDINGS

For busy women, the Sweet Endings of a meal seem like pie in the sky. But it's a myth that anything made with flour takes hours. Desserts can be easy and done ahead. Just mark your calendars as a day off from computing calories! Also, bake some oven lovin' for great gifts. Sweets from the heart and compliments from the chef don't come any kinder.

Desserts can't count as sweet nothings as long as cream and sugar, eggs and butter weigh a sweet something. But if you want to have your pound cake and eat it too, dine lightly at dinner, forget thick or thinner. Diet dangerously for an evening and splurge your senses on Sweet Endings.

After a gallery gathering, symphony celebration or charity ball, an elegant Dessert Buffet should be the coup de grâce. Black marble and mother-of-pearl, tuxedoes and truffles may define good taste, but the test rests with your guests' sweet tooth on trial. Chocolate connoisseurs will call for encores after sampling the frozen Chocolate Moussecake or the definitely different White Chocolate Layer Cake. Even calorie critics will applaud the Amaretto Soufflé or sweet-tasting Cheese Spread, tingling with Grand Marnier.

If being at home on your range is more cozy, serve your guests a collection of Country Classic Desserts. Take a sentimental journey through your cupboard or attic to find quilts and gadgets, doilies and baskets, but don't serve antiques like plain apple pie for dessert. Introduce a new tradition such as Rum Apple Rings or Coconut Cream Cheesecake. Our Cranberry Cobbler is a new version of Grandma's Impossibly Easy Pie. When it cooks, the batter makes its own crust! If there's proof in the pudding that the evening was a success, the evidence will have disappeared along with the Blueberry Bread, an old-fashioned pudding spiced up with orange marmalade and lemon zest.

If you can't bake a dessert for a grand finale, give a good-bye chocolate (for under the pillow) to a favorite friend or steady fellow.

All good things must come to a sweet ending, and so from the Junior League of Dallas, we wish you happy trails and tasty tales from recipes and recollections SOUTH OF THE FORK.

SWEET ENDINGS

COUNTRY CLASSICS

RUM APPLE RINGS
p. 108

POACHED CHERRIES
p. 189

PEACH SUNDAE SAUCE
p. 108

BLUEBERRY BREAD PUDDING
p. 109

CRANBERRY COBBLER
p. 109

COCONUT CREAM CHEESECAKE
p. 108

PEANUT BRITTLE
p. 109

TRIPLE CHOCOLATE PEANUT CLUSTERS
p. 109

LATE EVENING DESSERT BUFFET

WHITE CHOCOLATE LAYER CAKE
p. 188

COLD AMARETTO SOUFFLÉ
p. 112

CHOCOLATE MOUSSECAKE
p. 112

GRAND MARNIER CHEESE BALL
p. 113

CREME CAMEMBERT
p. 193

ORANGE PECANS
p. 113

CHOCOLATE TRUFFLES
p. 189

LEMON CURD CAKE
p. 113

COUNTRY CLASSICS

RUM APPLE RINGS

POACHED CHERRIES

PEACH SUNDAE SAUCE

BLUEBERRY BREAD PUDDING

CRANBERRY COBBLER

COCONUT CREAM CHEESECAKE

PEANUT BRITTLE

TRIPLE CHOCOLATE PEANUT
CLUSTERS

RUM APPLE RINGS

1	pound apples, peeled and cored
2	Tablespoons rum
2	Tablespoons sugar
2	cups flour
3	Tablespoons sugar
½	teaspoon grated lemon peel
1	cup beer or white wine
2	teaspoons olive oil
	powdered sugar (optional)
	cinnamon (optional)

Preheat oven to 150°. Slice apples into ½-inch rounds. Sprinkle with rum and 2 Tablespoons sugar. Let stand a few minutes. In a large bowl, mix flour, 3 Tablespoons sugar, peel and beer or wine to form a batter. In a heavy, medium skillet, heat oil. Coat apples in batter and fry in oil until light brown on both sides. Do not crowd apples, adding more oil if necessary. Transfer apples to a baking dish. Sprinkle with powdered sugar and cinnamon if desired. Place in oven and keep warm until all slices are cooked. May also be served cold. *Serves 6.*

PEACH SUNDAE SAUCE

4	peaches, crushed and peeled (2 cups)
½	cup sugar
½	cup fresh orange juice
2	teaspoons fresh lemon juice
1	teaspoon vanilla extract (optional)
3	drops Angostura bitters

In a 1½-quart saucepan, mix peaches, sugar and orange juice. Stir over high heat until sugar dissolves and mixture boils. Reduce heat and simmer uncovered until thickened, 20 minutes. Remove from heat. Stir in remaining ingredients. Serve warm or cold over vanilla ice cream. *Serves 6.*

COCONUT CREAM CHEESECAKE

Crust

⅔	cup flour
1	Tablespoon sugar
5	Tablespoons chilled butter, cut into small pieces

Filling

3	8-ounce packages cream cheese, room temperature	1	cup whipping cream
1½	cups sugar	1	teaspoon fresh lemon juice
4	eggs, room temperature	½	teaspoon vanilla extract
2	egg yolks, room temperature	½	teaspoon almond extract
2	cups flaked coconut		toasted coconut (optional)

To prepare crust: Preheat oven to 325°. In a large bowl, combine flour and sugar. Using pastry blender or two knives, cut in butter until mixture resembles coarse meal. Shape into a ball and wrap in plastic. Chill 15 minutes. Press dough into the bottom of a 10-inch springform pan. Bake 15-20 minutes or until golden brown. Cool slightly.

To prepare filling: Preheat oven to 300°. In a large bowl, beat cheese and sugar until smooth. Beat in eggs and yolks, one at a time. Mix in coconut, cream, juice, vanilla and almond extract. Pour into slightly cooled crust. Bake 1 hour and 10 minutes or until filling edges are firm. Remove from oven and cool completely. Remove sides of pan. Cover cake with plastic wrap and chill at least 4 hours. To serve, sprinkle with toasted coconut and slice. *Serves 12.*

Wine Selection: Champagne

CRANBERRY COBBLER

2	cups fresh, whole cranberries	1	cup sugar
½	scant cup sugar	¾	cup shortening, melted
½	cup coarsely chopped pecans	1	cup flour
		½	cup butter, melted
2	eggs, beaten		whipped cream

Preheat oven to 325°. Combine berries, ½ cup sugar and pecans. Spread on bottom of a well-greased quiche or pie pan. In a large bowl, beat eggs with remaining sugar. Add shortening, flour and butter. Beat well. Pour batter over berries. Bake 1 hour. To serve, cut into pie-shaped wedges. Serve warm or at room temperature with whipped cream. *Serves 6-8.*

PEANUT BRITTLE

2	cups sugar	1	teaspoon vanilla
1	cup white corn syrup	⅓	stick margarine
½	cup water	1	heaping teaspoon
2	cups raw peanuts		baking soda

In a large heavy pot, bring sugar, corn syrup and water to a boil. Continue cooking until mixture reaches 234° on a candy thermometer (soft ball stage). Add peanuts. Continue cooking until mixture reaches 300° on candy thermometer (hard crack). Immediately remove from heat and add remaining ingredients. Mix quickly. Pour onto oiled cookie sheet. When cool enough to handle, about 2 minutes, pull it thin, using a spatula underneath and fingers on top. Pull as thinly as possible. When completely cooled, break into pieces. Store in tightly covered tin. *Makes 1 pound.*

BLUEBERRY BREAD PUDDING

12-14	slices firm-type bread	3	eggs, beaten lightly
½	cup butter, softened	¾	cup sugar
1½	cups fresh blueberries	3	Tablespoons Grand Marnier or Cointreau
2½	cups milk		
½	cup fresh orange juice		pinch of salt
2	teaspoons grated orange peel	½	cup orange marmalade

Remove crusts from bread. Spread with butter and arrange a single layer of 6-7 slices in a greased rectangular deep baking dish. Sprinkle with one-half of the blueberries. Make another layer with the remaining bread, buttered-side down. Cover with remaining berries. Set aside. In a large bowl, mix milk, juice, peel, eggs, sugar, 1 Tablespoon Grand Marnier and salt until well blended. Pour over bread mixture. Cover with cloth and let set at least 2 hours or up to 12. When ready to serve, preheat oven to 350°. In a small saucepan, melt marmalade with remaining liqueur. Brush on top of bread mixture. Place baking pan in larger pan. Fill with enough hot water to come halfway up the sides of the pan. Bake 1 hour. Serve warm or cold. *Serves 8.*

TRIPLE CHOCOLATE PEANUT CLUSTERS

2	pounds white chocolate	1	12-ounce package milk chocolate chips
1	12-ounce package semisweet chocolate chips	1	24-ounce jar unsalted, dry roasted peanuts

In top of double boiler, melt all chocolates, stirring constantly. Cool 5 minutes. Stir in peanuts. Drop mixture by Tablespoonfuls onto waxed paper. If chocolate begins to harden, it may be remelted in microwave. Let cool completely. Wrap in plastic and refrigerate until ready to serve. *Makes 7 dozen.*

LATE EVENING DESSERT BUFFET

WHITE CHOCOLATE LAYER CAKE

COLD AMARETTO SOUFFLÉ

CHOCOLATE MOUSSECAKE

GRAND MARNIER CHEESE BALL

CRÈME CAMEMBERT

ORANGE PECANS

CHOCOLATE TRUFFLES

LEMON CURD CAKE

COLD AMARETTO SOUFFLÉ

1 *dozen ladyfingers*	*¾ cup sugar*
½ cup cold water	*1 Tablespoon fresh lemon*
1 envelope unflavored	*juice*
gelatin	*1 cup whipping cream*
¾ cup Amaretto liqueur	*toasted slivered almonds*
6 eggs, separated and	
room temperature	

Make a collar for a 7-inch soufflé dish by tying a double thickness of waxed paper around the outside of the dish with kitchen string. The collar should extend 2½ inches above the rim of the dish. Butter the inside surface of the waxed paper (this is easier if paper is buttered before being tied around the dish). Split ladyfingers in half, lengthwise and stand upright around the inside of the dish, good side out (ladyfingers should touch, but not overlap - bottoms can be trimmed flat if necessary).

Pour cold water into a small heat-proof bowl and sprinkle gelatin over top. Let stand for 5 minutes. Set bowl in pan of simmering water and stir until gelatin is dissolved. Remove from heat and blend in liqueur. Let cool. Refrigerate, stirring occasionally, until slightly thickened, about 30 minutes.

In a large bowl, beat egg yolks until frothy. Gradually add ¼ cup sugar and beat until mixture is thick and lemon-colored. Add gelatin mixture and beat until light. In another large bowl, beat egg whites until soft peaks form. Gradually beat in remaining ½ cup sugar. Add lemon juice and beat until whites are stiff, but not dry.
In a small bowl, whip cream until soft peaks form. Gently fold whites into yolk mixture. Fold in cream. Carefully spoon mixture into prepared soufflé dish, smoothing top. Chill until firm, about 3 hours. To serve, remove collar and sprinkle with almonds. *Serves 6.*

CHOCOLATE MOUSSECAKE

12 ounces semisweet	*½ cup hazelnuts, toasted*
chocolate	*and finely chopped*
12 Tablespoons unsalted	*1 cup whipping cream*
butter	*4 ounces semisweet*
9 eggs, separated	*chocolate*
1 cup sugar	
2 Tablespoons hazelnut	
liqueur (optional)	

Preheat oven to 350°. Melt 12 ounces chocolate and butter in the top of a double boiler over simmering water. In a large bowl, beat egg yolks and sugar until light and lemon-colored. Add chocolate, liqueur and hazelnuts to egg mixture and mix well. In another large bowl, beat egg whites to hold stiff peaks. Completely incorporate 1 cup of egg whites into chocolate mixture, then gently fold chocolate mixture into remaining egg whites.

Pour one-half of mixture into 8-inch spring form pan. Refrigerate remaining mousse mixture. Bake cake for 26 minutes or until it puffs in center. Allow cake to cool in the pan for 30 minutes (it will sink in the middle). Whip cream until thick and fold into remaining mousse mixture. Spread on top of cake in spring form pan.
With a vegetable peeler, make chocolate curls from remaining 4-ounces of chocolate and place on top of cake. Cover with plastic wrap and freeze. To serve, thaw cake in refrigerator for 2 to 3 hours. Remove outside rim of pan. *Serves 10-12.*

Wine Selection: Texas Port or Champagne

LEMON CURD CAKE

Cake		Lemon Curd	
1	cup unsalted butter, softened	4	eggs
2	cups sugar	2	cups sugar
4	eggs, separated	4	Tablespoons unsalted butter
1	teaspoon vanilla		juice of 4 large lemons
3	cups sifted cake flour		grated zest of 4 lemons
2	teaspoons baking powder		
1	cup milk		
pinch of salt			

To prepare cake: Preheat oven to 350°. Butter and flour 2 9-inch cake pans. Cut waxed paper to fit the bottom of the pans. Butter and flour the paper. In large bowl of electric mixer, cream butter and sugar. In a medium bowl, beat egg yolks and vanilla. Gradually add to creamed mixture. Sift flour and baking powder together. Alternately add flour and milk to cake batter, beginning and ending with flour and beating well after each addition.

In a separate bowl, beat egg whites with a pinch of salt until stiff. Fold egg whites into batter and pour into prepared cake pans. Bake for 35 to 40 minutes or until cake begins to shrink away from the sides of the pans. Cool in pans for 5 minutes, then turn out on racks and cool completely. Spread one-third of lemon curd on top of one layer. Top with second layer and frost top and sides with remaining lemon curd.

To prepare Lemon Curd: In the top of a double boiler, beat eggs until blended. Add remaining ingredients. Place over simmering water and stir until well combined. Cook, stirring occasionally for 45 minutes. Remove from heat and cool completely (chill if time permits) before frosting cake. Lemon curd can be prepared 2 days in advance and refrigerated.

GRAND MARNIER CHEESE BALL

4	8-ounce packages cream cheese, softened	½	cup Grand Marnier
2	Tablespoons vanilla	¼	cup brown sugar
1	1-pound box powdered sugar		strawberries

In an electric mixer or food processor fitted with metal blade, beat cream cheese, vanilla, sugar and Grand Marnier until fluffy. Mound mixture into a round ball on a serving platter or line a decorative mold with plastic wrap and mold mixture. Refrigerate several hours and gently remove plastic wrap. The cheese ball will remain semi-soft. To serve, sprinkle brown sugar over top and surround with strawberries. Serve with dessert crackers such as wheat meal. *Serves 60-75.*

ORANGE PECANS

2	cups light brown sugar	1	pound pecan halves
½	cup milk		grated zest of 1 orange
1	Tablespoon vinegar		

In a medium saucepan, blend sugar and milk. Heat for 2 to 3 minutes. Stir in vinegar. Bring mixture to a boil. Cook until it reaches soft ball stage (234° on candy thermometer). Place pecans in large bowl. Pour hot mixture over them. Add grated orange zest. Stir until nuts are thoroughly coated. Spread pecans on waxed paper to dry. Store in airtight tin. *Makes 4 cups.*

APPETIZERS

SKEWERED GARLIC SHRIMP

1½	pounds large shrimp, peeled and deveined	1	Tablespoon parsley, chopped
2	Tablespoons olive oil	½	teaspoon salt
2	Tablespoons oil		pepper
1	teaspoon garlic, finely minced		lemon wedges
½	cup dry, unflavored bread crumbs		

Pat shrimp dry on paper towels. In a large bowl, mix oils and garlic and toss. Add bread crumbs, parsley, salt and pepper, tossing until shrimp is well coated. Let shrimp set in coating for 20 minutes to 1 hour at room temperature. Preheat broiler. Thread shrimp on skewers and broil 4 inches from heat for 3 to 4 minutes on each side until golden brown. Serve with lemon wedges. *Serves 4.*

SHRIMP WITH CABBAGE AND CAVIAR

18	large shrimp, peeled and deveined	2	cups heavy cream
	salt and white pepper	2	Tablespoons red salmon caviar
4	cups cabbage, finely shredded	3	Tablespoons butter

Season shrimp with salt and pepper. In a large skillet, melt butter and sauté shrimp for about 1 minute. Transfer shrimp to a plate and keep warm.

Add cabbage to the same skillet and sauté for 10 seconds. Add the cream and bring to a boil. Reduce the cabbage-cream mixture over medium heat until slightly thickened.

To serve: Place cabbage in a large serving dish or divide among 6 plates. Arrange shrimp on top of the cabbage and top with the remaining sauce. Sprinkle with caviar. *Serves 6.*

CRAB PUFFS

Puff Pastry

½	cup butter	1	cup flour, sifted
1	cup boiling water	4	eggs
½	teaspoon salt		

Crab Filling

6	ounces fresh lump crabmeat	1½	teaspoons prepared horseradish
8	ounces cream cheese, softened	1	teaspoon onion, minced

To prepare pastry: Preheat oven to 425°. In a medium saucepan, combine butter and boiling water. Heat until butter melts. Add salt and flour all at once. Stir vigorously until mixture forms a ball, about 2 minutes. Remove from heat. Add eggs, one at a time, beating until mixture is perfectly smooth and glossy. Drop by teaspoonfuls 2 inches apart on greased cookie sheets. Bake for 20-25 minutes or until golden. Turn off oven and leave door cracked. Prick puffs with a fork and return to oven for 20 minutes to dry centers.

To prepare filling: In a small mixing bowl, combine crabmeat, cream cheese, horseradish and onion. Blend well.

To assemble: Slice tops off cooled puffs and fill with crab mixture. Replace tops and serve. *Makes 18-24 puffs.*

To save fresh basil for out-of-season use, finely chop basil in food processor with a small amount of olive oil. Drop mixture by tablespoons onto waxpaper-lined cookie sheets. Freeze basil until firm and place in plastic bags. All winter you have pre-measured fresh basil to use.

SPINACH TARTS

Pastry

1	3-ounce package cream cheese, softened	½	cup butter, softened
		1½	cups flour

Filling

1	10-ounce package frozen chopped spinach, cooked and drained	1	cup crumbled feta cheese or grated Romano cheese
1	egg, beaten	4	Tablespoons butter, melted
¼	teaspoon salt		
⅛	teaspoon pepper	2	Tablespoons grated Romano cheese
2	Tablespoons chopped onion		diced pimiento

To prepare pastry: In a medium bowl, combine cream cheese and butter. Add flour. Shape into 30 1-inch round balls and press into ungreased miniature muffin tins. Set aside.

To prepare tarts: Preheat oven to 350°. In a medium bowl, combine spinach, egg, salt, pepper, onion, cheese and butter blending well. Fill each tartlet shell with 1 heaping teaspoon of mixture and sprinkle with Romano cheese. Bake for 30 minutes. Cool slightly before lifting from pans. Garnish each tart with pimiento. *Makes 30 tarts.*

Chilling onions decreases the tears when slicing or chopping.

LIPTAUER SPREAD

8	ounces cream cheese, softened	1	teaspoon capers
2	Tablespoons anchovy paste	½	teaspoon salt
			radicchio leaves
3	Tablespoons sour cream		roasted red peppers
½	cup unsalted butter, softened		hard-boiled egg whites, chopped
1	Tablespoon Dijon mustard		hard-boiled egg yolks, chopped
1½	Tablespoons paprika		red onion, chopped
			red or black caviar

In a large bowl, combine cream cheese, anchovy paste, sour cream, butter, mustard, paprika, capers and salt. Pour mixture into a 2½ cup mold lined with plastic wrap and chill at least 24 hours. To serve, unmold onto platter and surround with radicchio leaves filled with garnishes. Serve with toast triangles or cocktail rye bread. *Serves 15.*

MINTED LIME SHRIMP

Dressing   *Salad*

1	cup fresh lime juice (6 large limes)	1	head Boston lettuce
¼	cup salad oil	¾	cup feta cheese, crumbled
½	cup sugar	¾	cup fresh mint, chopped
2	dozen shrimp, unpeeled		

To prepare dressing: In a small bowl, mix all ingredients. Chill. To prepare salad: Grill shrimp 5 minutes, turning once. Take from fire and cool. Remove shells but leave tails on. Chill. When ready to serve, tear lettuce into bite-size pieces and place on individual salad plates. Put shrimp on top, forming a circle with tails inside. Spoon on dressing and sprinkle with cheese and mint. *Serves 4-6.*

PICADILLY DIP

½	pound ground beef	¾	cup diced pimiento
½	pound hot bulk pork sausage	¾	cup sliced almonds, toasted
3	green onions, white parts and ¼ green part, sliced	1	6-ounces tomato paste
		2	jalapeños, chopped
2	cloves garlic, minced	¾	cup raisins
4	tomatoes, peeled and chopped	1	teaspoon powdered oregano
3	medium potatoes, cooked and coarsely chopped	2	teaspoons chili powder
		1	teaspoon salt
		1	teaspoon pepper
		2	cups water

In a large saucepan, brown beef and sausage with onions and garlic. Add remaining ingredients and cook over low heat for 1 hour. Serve from a chafing dish with tortilla chips. *Serves 20.*

STACKED CRÊPES

¾	cup mayonnaise	¾	pound fresh spinach, rinsed and trimmed
¼	cup green onions (green and white parts), thinly sliced	¾	pound salami, thinly sliced
¼	cup Dijon mustard	¾	pound Monterey Jack cheese, thinly sliced
24	crêpes		

In a small bowl, combine mayonnaise, onions and mustard. Set aside. Lay one crêpe on a board and spread with mayonnaise mixture. Place layer of salami over mayonnaise mixture. Top with another crêpe. Spread second crêpe with mayonnaise mixture and top with a layer of spinach. Place a third crêpe over spinach, spread with mayonnaise mixture and top with a layer of cheese. Repeat all three layers and top with a crêpe. Make 2 more stacks with remaining ingredients. Wrap in plastic wrap and chill up to 24 hours. To serve, stick 8 toothpicks around each stack at regular intervals and cut into 8 wedges. *Makes 24 wedges.*

CRAB QUESADILLAS

⅓	cup unsalted butter	½	cup onion, chopped
¼	cup safflower oil	¼	cup mayonnaise
1	clove garlic, minced	1	teaspoon salt
1	chili poblano, roasted, peeled, and diced; or 2 jalapeño peppers, stemmed, seeded and finely diced	1	Tablespoon chopped cilantro
		⅓	cup pepper-jack cheese (Monterey Jack with jalapeño peppers)
1	pound lump crabmeat	16	flour tortillas

Garlic's flavor becomes milder as it cooks. Also, the fresher the garlic, the milder its taste.

Preheat oven to 475°. Heat butter and oil in a medium saucepan to melt. Pour all but 2 Tablespoons in a small cup and reserve. Add garlic and onion to remaining butter and oil and sauté over medium heat. Remove from heat and stir in chilies, crab, mayonnaise, salt and cilantro. Mix well. Lay the tortillas on a heated baking sheet and brush liberally with the reserved butter and oil. Turn on the opposite side. Spread the crab mixture on half the tortilla. Top with a spoonful of cheese and fold over. Repeat with remaining tortillas. Bake quesadillas until tops are golden and filling is hot, about 2-4 minutes. Cut in quarters to serve. *Serves 8.*

CAVIAR SOUFFLÉ

2	Tablespoons unsalted butter		finely grated zest of 1 lemon
3	Tablespoons flour	2	Tablespoons vodka pepper
1	cup half-and-half	8	egg whites, room temperature
4	egg yolks		pinch of salt
½	cup golden or American salmon caviar	¼	teaspoon cream of tartar
⅓	cup snipped fresh chives		

Preheat oven to 400°. In a medium saucepan, melt butter until foamy. Add flour and cook, stirring for 1 minute. Gradually add half-and-half, stirring constantly until thick and smooth. Remove from heat and add egg yolks, one at a time, mixing well after each addition. Add caviar, chives, lemon zest, vodka and pepper. Beat egg whites with salt until foamy. Add cream of tartar and continue to beat until soft peaks form. Fold whites into sauce and pour into a 6-cup buttered soufflé dish. Bake 15 to 20 minutes until puffed and golden. Serve immediately. Soufflé will be soft and slightly runny. *Serves 6 as a first course.*

TORTILLA PIZZAS

20	flour tortillas	2	cups cooked chicken (preferably grilled), shrimp or beef fajita meat cut in small pieces
10	Tablespoons picante sauce		
¼	cup butter, melted		
20	Tablespoons picante sauce	1	red pepper, diced
10	Tablespoons grated Parmesan cheese	1	green pepper, diced
2½	cups grated Mozzarella or Monterey Jack cheese	3	Tablespoons chopped cilantro or fresh basil

Put 10 tortillas on a cookie sheet and sprinkle lightly with water. Spread 1 Tablespoon picante sauce on each one. Sprinkle remaining tortillas lightly with water on one side, then put on top of tortillas on cookie sheet pressing wet sides together so they stick. Brush with melted butter. Preheat the broiler and lightly brown tortillas on both sides. Remove from oven.

Preheat to 450°. Spread 2 Tablespoons picante sauce on each tortilla base. Top each with 1 Tablespoon Parmesan cheese and 2 Tablespoons grated cheese. Evenly sprinkle chicken and peppers over cheese. Top with cilantro or basil. Sprinkle 2 Tablespoons additional grated cheese on each and bake 8 to 10 minutes until cheese is melted and lightly browned. Cut in wedges. *Serves 10.*

Tip for grilling chicken: put bone side down next to the heat. The bones act as an insulator and keeps chicken from browning too fast.

ARTICHOKES WITH CURRY SAUCE

3	egg yolks	1	teaspoon Dijon mustard
1	Tablespoon lemon juice		
2	Tablespoons water	1/2	cup hot melted butter
1/4	teaspoon salt	4	large artichokes,
1/8	teaspoon curry powder		steamed

In blender or food processor fitted with metal blade, combine egg yolks, lemon juice, water, salt, curry powder and mustard and process very briefly. With machine running, pour butter in a steady stream and blend on high for 30 seconds. Serve immediately with cold or warm artichokes. *Serves 4.*

CAPONATA

1/4	cup olive oil	2	Tablespoons capers
1 1/2	pounds eggplant, cut in 1-inch cubes	2	teaspoons salt
		1/2	teaspoon pepper
2	large onions, diced	2	teaspoons chopped fresh basil
2	large green peppers, cut in 1-inch pieces		
		1/3	cup red wine vinegar
2	cloves garlic, minced	1/2	cup chopped parsley
1	28-ounce can Italian plum tomatoes, undrained	2	Tablespoons tomato paste
		1/2	cup black olives
2	Tablespoons sugar	1/2	cup pine nuts, toasted

In a dutch oven, combine oil, eggplant, onions, peppers, garlic and tomatoes over medium-low heat and cook 20 to 30 minutes until tender. Add remaining ingredients except pine nuts. Cover and simmer for 15 minutes. Remove from heat and stir in pine nuts. Serve at room temperature or cold. *Serves 10 to 12.*

STUFFED ARTICHOKES

4	artichokes, steamed, halved, cored	3/4	pound mushrooms, thinly sliced
3/4	pound cooked salad shrimp, crab or lobster		Vinaigrette

Vinaigrette

1 1/2	Tablespoons shallots, minced	3	Tablespoons lemon juice
1 1/2	teaspoons salt	3	Tablespoons white wine vinegar
3/4	teaspoon dried tarragon		
		8	Tablespoons vegetable oil
3	egg yolks		
3	teaspoons Dijon mustard	4	Tablespoons olive oil
			pepper

To prepare appetizer: Place each artichoke half on a plate and fill the center with combined shrimp and mushrooms. Cover with vinaigrette. *Serves 8.*

To prepare vinaigrette: In a small bowl, mix shallots with salt and tarragon. Using a wire whisk, beat in the egg yolks, then the mustard, lemon juice and vinegar. Add combined oils in a steady stream, whisking until well incorporated. Sprinkle top with pepper.

Note: Leaves of artichoke may be dipped in vinaigrette.

"Educated women make the best wives; they may not be good cooks, but they find more ways to explain why dinner isn't ready."

MUSHROOMS STUFFED WITH GOAT CHEESE

8	large mushrooms	½	teaspoon chopped fresh
1	Tablespoon unsalted		thyme, basil, tarragon
	butter		or dill
¼	cup finely chopped	¼	teaspoon salt
	onion		pinch of pepper
4	ounces mild goat cheese	3	Tablespoons olive oil

Preheat oven to 425°. Separate mushroom stems from caps. Finely chop stems and set aside caps. In a small skillet, melt butter over low heat and sauté onion until translucent. Add mushroom stems and cook until liquid evaporates, about 3 minutes. Remove from heat and add cheese, mixing well. Season with salt, pepper and herbs. Brush mushroom caps with olive oil. Fill with cheese mixture. Place on baking sheet and drizzle with remaining olive oil. Bake 10 minutes or until lightly browned. *Serves 4.*

MANGO AND GREEN CHILI QUESADILLAS

1	yellow onion, thinly sliced	2	mangoes, peeled and diced
1	Tablespoon lime juice	¼	cup unsalted butter, melted
10	flour tortillas		
8	ounces Brie cheese, thinly sliced	¼	cup safflower oil
4	poblano chilies, roasted, peeled, seeded and diced		

Preheat oven to 475°. In a small saucepan, cook onion and lime juice in water to cover for 2 to 3 minutes. Drain, rinse with cold water and drain again. On one half of each tortilla, arrange 1/10 of the cheese, chilies and mango. Fold tortillas in half. Brush both sides with the butter and oil mixture and place on cookie sheet. Quesadillas can be prepared to this point one day in advance and refrigerated. To serve, bring to room temperature before baking for 3-4 minutes, turning once. Cut each into thirds. *Makes 30.*

OYSTERS ROCKEFELLER

1	bunch green onions, cut in 2-inch lengths	½	cup fine bread crumbs, toasted
1	bunch celery, cut in 2-inch lengths	¼	cup Worcestershire sauce
1	bunch parsley	1	ounce Pernod
2	10-ounce packages frozen, chopped spinach, cooked and drained	½	teaspoon anise seed
			salt and pepper
			cayenne pepper
1½	pounds butter, melted	6	dozen oysters, shucked

Preheat oven to 350°. In food processor fitted with metal blade, combine onions, celery, parsley, spinach and butter. Process until puréed. Remove to a large bowl and add bread crumbs, Worcestershire sauce, Pernod, anise seed, salt, pepper and cayenne pepper to taste. Place oysters on a bed of rock salt in the oven until puffed and curled (if using oysters in jar, place in a greased casserole 2 inches apart). Remove from oven and top with sauce. Preheat broiler and broil oysters until bubbly. Serve with lemon wedges. *Serves 12.*

CREAMY CHICKEN LIVER PÂTÉ

1 cup chicken stock	1 clove garlic, crushed
½ pound boneless, skinless chicken breasts	1½ teaspoons salt
	½ teaspoon nutmeg
½ pound chicken livers	¼ teaspoon ground cloves
½ cup chopped onions	large pinch cayenne pepper
4 eggs, hard-boiled	¾ cup unsalted butter, softened
2 Tablespoons lemon juice	½ cup whipping cream, whipped
1 Tablespoon Dijon mustard	

Place chicken breasts and stock in a saucepan. Cover and cook over medium-high heat for 10 minutes or until chicken is tender. Add livers; continue cooking for 5 minutes or until livers barely lose their pinkness. Discard broth. In food processor or blender, grind meat very fine. Add all other ingredients except cream; blend until very smooth. Place in a medium-size bowl and chill 30 minutes. Fold in cream. Transfer to a serving dish and chill, preferably overnight to allow flavors to develop. Serve on Belgian endive leaves. *Serves 12.*

Note: Should be prepared 1 day in advance.

When making stocks, if the water evaporates, always add cold water (never warm).

CRAB AND ROASTED PEPPERS

1 red bell pepper	⅛ teaspoon cayenne pepper
2 Anaheim peppers	
½ cup finely chopped onion	1 teaspoon salt
	½ pound fresh crabmeat, shells removed
2 Tablespoons butter, melted	
	½ French baguette, thinly sliced into 24 pieces
1 cup whipping cream	
3 ounces cream cheese	4 Tablespoons butter, melted
4 Tablespoons grated Romano cheese	
	4 sun-dried tomatoes, drained and diced
⅛ teaspoon white pepper	

On a broiler pan, roast peppers 4 inches from heat, turning every 5 minutes until peppers are charred. Seal peppers in a plastic bag and place in freezer for 15 minutes. In a medium skillet, sauté onions in 2 Tablespoons melted butter. Add cream and bring to a boil. Continue to cook until liquid is reduced to ½ cup. Blend in cream cheese, Romano cheese and seasonings. Set aside.

Preheat oven to 350°. Remove peppers from freezer and peel skins by running under water. Remove stems and seeds and chop peppers finely. Gently fold peppers and crabmeat into cream mixture. Reserve. Brush 4 Tablespoons melted butter on both sides of bread slices. Bake on baking sheet for 10 minutes. Remove bread slices and mound 1 Tablespoon crabmeat mixture on each one. Top each bread slice with a sliver of sun-dried tomato and bake for 10 more minutes. Serve immediately. *Makes 24 hors d'oeuvres.*

The Spanish have had an influence on Texas cuisine since 1528 when Cabeza De Vaca shipwrecked on Texas shores. It was recorded in 1690 that Spanish missionaries dined on tamales.

PHYLLO TRIANGLES WITH SAUSAGE-MUSHROOM FILLING

Filling

4 Tablespoons unsalted butter, melted	1 very large onion, chopped medium-fine
½ cup minced shallots	1 Tablespoon vegetable oil
1 pound fresh mushrooms, chopped medium-fine	1 pound sausage meat
1½ teaspoons salt	1 teaspoon salt
¼ teaspoon pepper	¼ teaspoon pepper
6 Tablespoons sherry	3 Tablespoons sherry
4 slices bacon, cut into 1-inch pieces	2 Tablespoons chopped fresh parsley
16 sheets phyllo dough additional melted butter	1 cup sour cream

To prepare filling: In a large skillet, sauté shallots in butter until limp. Stir in mushrooms and continue cooking 2-3 minutes. Season with salt and pepper. Cook until liquid evaporates. Stir in sherry and cook until it evaporates. Transfer to a large bowl and set aside. Clean skillet, add bacon and fry until crisp. Drain, reserving 1 Tablespoon fat. Crumble bacon and stir into mushroom mixture. Sauté onion in reserved fat. Add to mushroom mixture. Clean skillet, heat oil and add sausage. Cook until most liquid evaporates. Drain off fat. Stir in salt, pepper and sherry. Cook over medium-high heat, stirring constantly, until liquid evaporates. Drain in colander lined with paper towels. Stir into mushroom mixture. Mix in parsley and sour cream. Set aside.

To prepare entrée-size triangles: Preheat oven to 375°. Using 4 phyllo sheets, brush each with butter. Cover first sheet with the 3 other sheets. Cut stack in half lengthwise, forming 2 rectangles. Spread ¾ cup filling on each rectangle. Fold dough like a flag, forming a triangle.

Place on greased baking sheet. Repeat with remaining phyllo sheets. Brush triangles with butter. Bake 35 minutes or until golden brown. *Makes 8 triangles.*

To prepare hors d'oeuvres-size triangles: Preheat oven to 375°. Using 4 phyllo sheets, brush each with butter. Cover first sheet with the 3 other sheets. Cut stack widthwise into 5 equal rectangles. Spread 1 Tablespoon filling on each rectangle. Follow entrée-size triangle directions for folding and preparing dough to bake. Bake 10 minutes or until golden brown. *Makes 48 triangles.*

Note: Triangles can be frozen. Do not thaw before baking. Place on lightly greased baking sheet. Brush with melted butter and bake at 375° for 45-50 minutes. For a variation, omit dough, triple sour cream and serve in a chafing dish as a dip.

SOUPS AND SALADS

WILD MUSHROOM SOUP

1	pound fresh wild mushrooms, finely chopped (cultivated mushrooms can be substituted)
	juice of 1 lemon
2	Tablespoons butter
1	shallot, chopped (or 2 Tablespoons chopped onion)
1	clove garlic, minced
	salt and white pepper
4	Tablespoons butter
5	Tablespoons flour
4½	cups beef stock
½	cup whipping cream

In a medium bowl, sprinkle mushrooms with lemon juice. Melt 2 Tablespoons butter in a large skillet and cook shallot and garlic until soft, but not brown. Add mushrooms and continue cooking, stirring occasionally, for about 45 minutes until juices have evaporated. Season with salt and pepper and set aside. Melt 4 Tablespoons butter in a large saucepan and stir in the flour. Add beef stock gradually, stirring continuously to avoid lumps. Simmer for 20 minutes. Add mushrooms and simmer 10 more minutes. Correct seasonings and add cream. Serve immediately. *Serves 6.*

OXTAIL SOUP

2	oxtails, trimmed of fat and cut into 2-inch lengths
6	quarts water
1	onion, chopped
1	bunch leeks, chopped
1	Tablespoon salt
1	teaspoon whole peppercorns
2	carrots, sliced
3	14½-ounce cans beef broth
1	1-pound can tomatoes
1	Tablespoon thyme
1	Tablespoon chopped parsley
1	potato, cubed
¾	cup barley
3	cloves garlic, pressed

In a large pot, bring oxtails and water to a boil. Skim. Add remaining ingredients except potato, barley and garlic. Cover and simmer 3 hours. Stir in remaining ingredients and cook 1 more hour. Correct seasonings. Serve hot. *Serves 8.*

SPINACH AND OYSTER SOUP

4	Tablespoons butter, melted
¼	cup onions, finely chopped
1	clove garlic, minced
4	Tablespoons flour
3	cups half-and-half cream
1	cup chicken broth
¾	cup uncooked, puréed spinach
1	pint oysters, chopped
	salt and pepper

In a large saucepan, sauté onion and garlic in butter over low heat. Add flour and cook 1 minute. Whisk in cream and cook until thickened. Stir in remaining ingredients. Bring to a boil. Cook until oysters curl slightly. Serve hot. *Serves 6-8.*

SQUASH SOUP

½	cup butter, melted	2	cups whipping cream
2½	cups chopped onions		garlic salt
4	cups sliced summer		white pepper
	squash		ground nutmeg
2	cups chicken broth		chopped parsley
¼	teaspoon sugar		chopped chives

In a large saucepan, sauté onions in butter. Add squash and broth. Cook over moderate-low heat until squash is tender. Stir in sugar. Transfer mixture to a blender or food processor and purée. Pour into a large bowl. Cool. Mix in cream. Season with spices to taste. Chill. May be served hot or cold. Garnish with parsley and chives. *Serves 4-6.*

Mixtures to be puréed for soups should be cooled slightly before being placed in the food processor or blender.

ZESTY ZUCCHINI SOUP

4	cups water	½	onion, sliced
7	chicken bouillon cubes	1	8-ounce package
6	zucchini (or carrots,		cream cheese, cubed
	broccoli, etc.), sliced		salt and pepper
2	carrots, sliced		hot sauce

In a non-aluminum large pot, bring 3 cups water to a boil. Stir in bouillon cubes until dissolved. Add vegetables, lower heat and simmer until vegetables are tender. Transfer mixture to a blender or food processor and purée. Pour into a large bowl and blend in cream cheese. Season to taste with remaining ingredients. If too thick, thin with water. Serve hot or cold. *Serves 4-6.*

GARDEN CREAM OF TOMATO SOUP

3	Tablespoons olive oil	¼	cup parsley, chopped
2	Tablespoons butter	2	Tablespoons fresh
1	carrot, finely diced		basil, chopped
1	green bell pepper, diced		salt and pepper
3	stalks celery, finely	2	cups half-and-half,
	diced		room temperature
2	medium onions, minced		chives, snipped
3½	pounds tomatoes, peeled and cut in large pieces		

In a dutch oven, heat oil and butter. Add carrots, bell pepper, celery and onions. Cook over low heat for 20 minutes until tender. Add tomatoes and continue to cook for 30 minutes. Stir in parsley, basil, salt and pepper. (Soup can be frozen at this point.) Add half-and-half and cook until heated thoroughly. Garnish with chives. *Serves 8.*

ENGLISH GARDEN SALAD

4	Tablespoons raspberry vinegar	8	slices bacon, cooked and crumbled
8	ounces mild Stilton cheese	1	bunch curly endive or escarole
6	slices purple onion, separated into rings	½	cup pine nuts
12	fresh mushrooms, sliced		

In a large skillet, warm vinegar over medium heat until slightly bubbly. Add cheese and stir until it begins to melt. Add onions and mushrooms. Cook 1 minute. Stir in remaining ingredients. Cook 1-2 minutes, tossing lightly until heated thoroughly. Serve immediately. *Serves 4-6.*

POSOLE

1	3-pound pork loin or shoulder, trimmed of fat	2	1 pound, 13-ounce cans white hominy, drained
3	cups chicken stock	1	cup tomatoes, chopped and peeled
1	onion, sliced	4	ounces mild green chilies, chopped
1	clove garlic, peeled		
½	teaspoon dried oregano	¼	cup fresh cilantro, chopped
	salt		
1	2½-pound chicken	2	avocados, diced
1	Tablespoon butter or bacon fat, melted	1	bunch green onions, chopped
2	onions, chopped		cream cheese, cut in tiny squares
2	cloves garlic, minced		
2	Tablespoons chili powder		corn tortillas, cut in thin strips and fried

In a large pot, place pork, 1 onion, garlic, oregano and salt in stock. Add enough water to cover meat. Bring to a boil. Lower heat and simmer 1 hour 15 minutes or until meat is tender. In a separate pot, place chicken and enough water to cover. Bring to a boil. Lower heat and simmer 45 minutes or until meat is tender. Remove meats. Strain stocks from both pots. Chill meats and stocks. To serve, remove fat from cold stock. Cut pork and chicken meat into ½-inch cubes. In a large pot, sauté remaining onions and garlic in butter. Stir in pork cubes and chili powder and cook several more minutes, stirring well. Add the reserved stock (about 8 cups), hominy, tomatoes, chilies and cilantro. Simmer 20 minutes. Add chicken cubes and cook 15 more minutes. Serve ladled into individual soup bowls with avocados, green onions, cream cheese and tortillas for garnish. *Serves 8.*

GUMBO

1	cup flour	1	Tablespoon pepper
¾	cup vegetable oil	1	Tablespoon chopped parsley
2	teaspoons salt		
2	green bell peppers, finely chopped	3	cups sliced fresh okra
2	large onions, finely chopped	1	Polish sausage, sliced
		3	pounds cooked bite-size chicken or turkey pieces
4	stalks celery, finely chopped		
6	14½-ounce cans chicken broth	1	bay leaf
		½	teaspoon cayenne pepper
1	8-ounce can tomato sauce		filé to taste
			cooked rice

In a large pot, make a roux by mixing flour, oil and salt. Cook over low heat until the mixture turns a deep brown. Stir in remaining ingredients except filé and rice. Cook at least 1 hour. Flavor improves the longer it simmers. When ready to serve, stir in filé. Serve in bowls, over rice. *Serves 8.*

Note: For shrimp gumbo, omit chicken and add 3 pounds fresh peeled shrimp 20 minutes before serving.

NAVAJO CORN SOUP

2	cups creamed corn	½	teaspoon pepper
2	cups half-and-half cream	¼	teaspoon mace
		¼	teaspoon Tabasco
1	cup celery with leaves, finely chopped		

In a large bowl, combine all ingredients. Serve hot or cold. *Serves 6-8.*

BLACK-EYED PEA SOUP

2 quarts water	½ cup chopped onions
2 cups black-eyed peas (dried or fresh)	2-4 Tablespoons chili powder
2 cups chopped celery	salt and pepper
1 pound ham hock	1 pound smoked sausage, sliced
3 cups chopped carrots	

In a large pot, combine all ingredients except sausage. Bring to a boil; reduce heat and simmer 3 hours or until peas are soft. Add sausages and cook 30 more minutes. Serve hot. *Serves 8-10.*

Note: If using dried peas, soak overnight and drain.

SHERRIED CREAM OF MUSHROOM SOUP

¼ cup butter, melted	3 Tablespoons flour
½ pound fresh mushrooms, sliced	1¾ cups chicken broth
⅓ cup finely chopped onions	¼ cup dry sherry
	salt
1 clove garlic, minced	¼ teaspoon white pepper
1 Tablespoon fresh lemon juice	2 cups half-and-half cream
	parsley

In a large saucepan, sauté mushrooms, onion and garlic in butter. Stir in lemon juice and flour. Gradually add broth, sherry and seasonings. Cook over low heat until slightly thickened, stirring constantly. (May be chilled at this point 2-3 hours prior to serving.) Stir in cream and cook until hot. Do not boil. Garnish with parsley. *Serves 4.*

GREEN PEA SOUP

1 quart water	6-7 cups chicken broth or water
¼ pound lean bacon (3-4 slices)	salt and pepper
3 Tablespoons butter	croutons
2 leeks, thinly sliced	6 parsley sprigs
1 large onion, thinly sliced	
3 pounds fresh green peas or 2 10-ounce boxes frozen peas	

In a saucepan, bring water to a boil. Add bacon and boil slowly for 10 minutes. Drain. In a large pot, melt butter. Add bacon, leeks and onion. Cover tightly and cook slowly over medium-low heat for 10 minutes without browning. Stir in peas and 6 cups broth, salt and pepper. Bring to a boil. Simmer 30-35 minutes or until peas are tender. Remove bacon and discard. Transfer mixture to a blender or food processor and purée. Strain through a fine-mesh sieve. Return to pot and bring to a boil, adding more stock if too thick. To serve, pour soup into tureen or individual bowls and garnish with croutons and parsley. *Serves 6.*

An easy way to store stocks is in ice cubes. After stock is cooled, refrigerate until fat congeals on top. Skim fat off of stock and freeze in ice cube trays. Store the cubes in plastic bags, making it easy to use as much or as little as you need.

AVOCADO AND SHRIMP SALAD WITH FRESH DILL

3	Tablespoons olive oil		juice of ½ lemon
2	Tablespoons white wine vinegar	2	Tablespoons dill, chopped
1	teaspoon Dijon mustard	2	Tablespoons chives, chopped
1	pound cooked shrimp, cubed		dill sprigs
2	avocados, cubed		lemon wedges

Dressing

½	cup mayonnaise		Tabasco sauce
1	Tablespoon chili sauce		salt and pepper
1	large clove garlic, crushed		

To prepare salad: In a medium bowl, whisk together olive oil, vinegar and mustard. Add shrimp, toss well, cover and marinate 2 hours. Sprinkle avocado cubes with lemon juice in a large bowl. Drain shrimp and add to avocados along with dill and chives. Fold in enough dressing to lightly coat shrimp-avocado mixture. Cover and chill. To serve, divide among salad plates and garnish with dill sprigs and lemon wedges. *Serves 4.*

To prepare dressing: In a small bowl, whisk dressing ingredients together until smooth. Chill until ready to assemble salad.

Never use plastic bowls when beating egg whites because they retain a greasy film which inhibits the volume of beaten egg whites.

PUEBLO CHICKEN SALAD

6	cooked chicken breast halves, skinned and boned	2	cloves garlic, finely chopped
½	cup extra virgin olive oil	1	small red onion, julienned
½	cup fresh lime juice	5	fresh green chilies, roasted and julienned
¼	teaspoon ground cumin	4	fresh Roma tomatoes, chopped
1	Tablespoon Durkees dressing		lettuce
	salt and white pepper		goat cheese medallions
1	small bunch fresh cilantro, finely chopped		pickled nopales (cactus)

In a large bowl, slice chicken into bite-size pieces. Add oil, lime juice, cumin, dressing, salt and pepper. Toss in cilantro, garlic, onion, chilies and tomatoes. Serve on a bed of lettuce garnished with cheese and nopales. *Serves 6.*

GREEN PEA SALAD

4	10-ounce packages frozen large peas, thawed and dried		salt and pepper
		1	cup sour cream
1½	pounds bacon, cooked and crumbled	2	bunches watercress, chopped
2	bunches green onions, finely chopped		

In a large bowl, combine peas, bacon, onions, seasonings to taste and sour cream. Chill up to 24 hours. To serve, toss with watercress. *Serves 8-10.*

DILLED GREEN BEANS WITH WALNUTS

Beans

4	cups fresh baby French green beans	½	cup walnuts or pecans

Marinade

⅔	cup safflower oil	¼	teaspoon dry mustard
1	Tablespoon lemon juice	⅛	teaspoon garlic, minced
⅓	cup red wine vinegar	1	Tablespoon tarragon, finely chopped (or ¼ teaspoon dried)
½-1	teaspoon salt		
¼	teaspoon white pepper		
2	Tablespoons dill, finely chopped (or 1 teaspoon dried)		

To prepare beans: Steam beans briefly, about 2-3 minutes, until bright green. Drain and cool. Pour marinade over beans and cover. Chill 12-24 hours. To serve, toss with nuts. *Serves 6-8.*

To prepare marinade: Combine all ingredients in a medium jar. Shake vigorously.

TOMATOES AL FRESCO

6-8	tomatoes, coarsely chopped	¼	cup fresh basil, chopped (or 2 Tablespoons dried)
¼	cup green onions, chopped		
¼	cup celery, chopped	¼	cup red wine vinegar
¼	cup capers, drained	½	cup olive oil
¼	cup parsley, chopped		salt and pepper

In a large bowl, combine all ingredients. Chill. *Serves 4-6.*

WARM CAESAR SALAD

Salad

2	Tablespoons unsalted butter	2	medium heads romaine lettuce
2	Tablespoons olive oil	¼	cup grated Parmesan cheese
1	8-ounce loaf Italian bread, cut into ¾-inch cubes		pepper
2	hard-boiled eggs, coarsely chopped		

Dressing

1½	Tablespoons anchovy paste	1	clove garlic, pressed
1	Tablespoon Worcestershire sauce	3	Tablespoons white wine vinegar
		⅔	cup olive oil

To prepare salad: In a medium skillet, melt butter with oil over moderate heat. When foam subsides, add bread and toss to coat. Reduce heat to low and sauté, stirring often, until croutons are crisp and golden brown, 5-7 minutes. Set aside. In a small bowl, force eggs through a sieve. Set aside. In a large bowl, tear romaine into bite-size pieces. Toss well with hot dressing. Add cheese and toss again. Divide salad among 6 plates. Sprinkle croutons on top. Spoon small mound of eggs in the centers. Season with pepper. Serve at once. *Serves 6.*

To prepare dressing: In a small saucepan, whisk together paste, Worcestershire, garlic and vinegar. Whisk in oil. Set in pan over moderate heat and bring to a boil. Immediately pour over salad.

GREEN SALAD WITH BLEU CHEESE VINAIGRETTE

Salad

1	small head Boston lettuce	½	bunch watercress, coarsely chopped
1	small head red leaf lettuce		

Dressing

1	clove garlic, minced	¼	cup olive oil
½	teaspoon Dijon mustard	½	cup vegetable oil
1½	teaspoons lemon juice	2	ounces bleu cheese, crumbled
1	Tablespoon red wine vinegar	½	teaspoon sugar

To prepare salad: Tear lettuces into bite-size pieces in a large bowl. Chill. Add watercress. Toss with dressing. Serve immediately. *Serves 4.*

To prepare dressing: Mix garlic, mustard, lemon juice and vinegar in a bowl. Add oils in a slow, steady stream, whisking rapidly. Stir in cheese and sugar.

Foods that are served chilled should be seasoned very generously as cooler temperatures deplete the punch of herbs and spices.

GREEN SALAD WITH BAKED GOAT CHEESE

Baked Cheese

2	4-ounce pieces Texas goat cheese		a few sprigs fresh herbs (rosemary, thyme, basil, etc.)
½	cup extra-virgin olive oil	1	cup bread crumbs

Dressing

	oil from marinade	2	Tablespoons balsamic vinegar
½	teaspoon Dijon mustard		salt and pepper

Salad

½	bunch watercress	1	loaf French bread, warmed
½	small head bibb lettuce		
1	small head radicchio or red lettuce		

To prepare cheese: Cut each piece of cheese into 2 rounds. Marinate in oil with sprigs of herbs at least 30 minutes. Preheat oven to 375°. Remove cheese from oil, reserving oil for dressing, and roll cheese in crumbs. Place on baking sheet and bake 10 minutes until golden. Serve warm.

To prepare dressing: Discard herbs from reserved oil and mix oil in a small bowl with mustard, vinegar and seasonings to taste.

To prepare salad: In a large bowl, tear watercress and lettuces into bite-size pieces. Toss with dressing. Arrange on individual salad plates. Place a round of baked cheese in center of each salad. Serve with bread. *Serves 4.*

CURRIED CHICKEN SALAD

Salad

2   Tablespoons peeled and diced apple
2   Tablespoons lemon juice
2½ cups cooked bite-size chicken pieces
2   cups red grapes, halved and seeded
1½ cups chopped celery

1½ cups sliced water chestnuts
3   Tablespoons chopped green onions
3   Tablespoons finely chopped parsley
1   Tablespoon chopped chutney
fresh fruit for garnish

Dressing

½   cup mayonnaise
½   cup sour cream
1   teaspoon grated onion

2   Tablespoons curry powder
salt and white pepper

To prepare salad: In a large bowl, sprinkle apple with lemon juice. Toss in remaining ingredients and dressing. Chill up to several days. Serve on a bed of lettuce garnished with fruit. *Serves 4-6.*

To prepare dressing: In a medium bowl, whisk all ingredients.

MIXED GREENS WITH SHALLOT VINAIGRETTE

Salad

¾   cup chopped walnuts
1   Tablespoon walnut oil or vegetable oil
1   head romaine lettuce, torn into bite-size pieces

1   head red leaf lettuce, torn into bite-size pieces
6   ounces grated Monterey Jack cheese

Vinaigrette

½   cup chopped parsley
2   large shallots
2   Tablespoons red wine vinegar
4   teaspoons Dijon mustard

1   teaspoon sugar
¼   teaspoon salt
pepper
⅔   cup vegetable oil
2   Tablespoons olive oil

To prepare salad: In a small skillet over low heat, sauté nuts in oil for 5 minutes. Drain on paper towels and reserve. Place lettuces, walnuts and cheese in a large salad bowl and toss with vinaigrette. *Serves 6.*

To prepare vinaigrette: Place parsley in food processor fitted with metal blade. With machine running, drop shallots through feed tube and mince. Add remaining ingredients and process briefly. Correct seasonings. Place in covered jar and set aside. Do not refrigerate.

SPINACH SALAD WITH BEETS AND PINE NUTS

Salad

1	pound fresh spinach, rinsed and trimmed	⅓	cup pine nuts or walnuts, toasted and cooled
1	8-ounce jar sliced beets, julienned		

Dressing

1	cup salad oil	3-4	Tablespoons finely chopped parsley
3	Tablespoons red wine vinegar	2	cloves garlic, crushed
4	Tablespoons sour cream	⅓	teaspoon salt
1	teaspoon sugar	⅔	teaspoon Dijon mustard

To prepare dressing: Mix all ingredients in a glass jar. Shake well. Refrigerate overnight.

To prepare salad: Divide the spinach among 8 salad plates. Sprinkle beets and pine nuts on each. To serve, remove garlic cloves from chilled dressing. Shake dressing well and drizzle over each salad. *Serves 8.*

ROQUEFORT DRESSING

3-4	Tablespoons chopped onions	½	teaspoon salt
2	cloves garlic, pressed	½	teaspoon pepper
1	cup sour cream	¼	teaspoon chopped fresh chives
2	cups mayonnaise		
1	Tablespoon sugar	4	ounces Roquefort or bleu cheese

In a food processor fitted with the metal blade, chop garlic. Add onion and sour cream blending well. Process in mayonnaise, sugar, salt, pepper, chives and half of the cheese. Add remaining cheese. Process until well blended. *Makes 3¼ cups.*

SPINACH SALAD WITH APPLES

Salad

1	pound fresh spinach, washed and trimmed	1	Tablespoon lemon juice
1	cup fresh bean sprouts, rinsed and drained	½	pound fresh mushrooms, sliced
1	Golden Delicious apple, cored and diced	6	slices bacon, cooked crisp and crumbled

Dressing

⅓	cup white wine vinegar	1	teaspoon salt
1	cup salad oil	1	teaspoon Worcestershire sauce
¼	cup onion, chopped		
¾	cup sugar		

To prepare salad: In a large bowl, tear spinach into bite-sized pieces. Add bean sprouts. Toss apple with lemon juice and add to spinach. Add remaining ingredients. To serve, toss with dressing. *Serves 8.*

To prepare dressing: Place ingredients in blender or food processor and blend well.

AVOCADO SALAD

3	avocados	1	Tablespoon lemon juice
¼	cup sour cream	½	teaspoon salt
2	tomatoes, chopped	6	slices bacon, cooked and crumbled
2	Tablespoons sliced green onions		

Halve avocados and carefully scoop out pulp, reserving shells. Dice avocado and add sour cream (more may be needed if avocados are not very ripe), tomatoes, green onions, lemon juice and salt. Carefully spoon mixture back into shells and top with crumbled bacon. *Serves 6.*

SNOW PEA SALAD

Salad

2	6-ounce packages frozen Chinese pea pods
salt	
1	cup cherry tomatoes, halved
8	ounces sliced water chestnuts, drained
1/4	cup green onions, chopped

Dressing

1/3	cup salad oil
1	Tablespoon lemon juice
1	Tablespoon white wine vinegar
1	small clove garlic, crushed
1/2	teaspoon salt
1/2	teaspoon sugar

To prepare salad: Cook peas in small amount of boiling, salted water until tender but still crisp, about 2 minutes. Drain and chill. To serve, in a large bowl combine peas, tomatoes, chestnuts and onions. Toss with dressing and serve immediately. *Serves 6-8.*

To prepare dressing: Mix together all ingredients until well blended.

"Like many other virtues, hospitality is practiced, in its perfection, by the poor. If the rich did their share, how the woes of the world would be lightened."
Mrs. Kirkland

HERB SAUCE FOR ARTICHOKES

Herb Sauce

1/2	cup red wine vinegar
1/2	cup butter, melted
1	cup olive oil
1	clove garlic, minced
1	teaspoon salt
1	teaspoon tarragon
1	teaspoon grated onion
1	teaspoon sugar
1	teaspoon dry mustard
	pepper
6	artichokes, cooked, trimmed, centers removed and chilled

To prepare sauce: In a small bowl, stir all ingredients until thoroughly blended. Let stand at room temperature at least one hour to blend flavors. Do not chill.

To serve: Fill artichokes with sauce. Serve immediately. *Serves 6.*

When using walnut oil or hazelnut oil in salad dressing, never use it alone; mix at least half with good vegetable oil or olive oil.

SALAD DRESSING WITH TOASTED SESAME SEEDS

3	Tablespoons sesame seeds
3/4	cup oil
1/4	cup vinegar
1/2	teaspoon sugar
1/4	cup grated Romano cheese
1	teaspoon salt
1/4	teaspoon pepper
1/4	teaspoon paprika

Preheat oven to 300°. Toast sesame seeds on baking sheet until lightly browned. In a small bowl, whisk seeds with remaining ingredients. Toss with salad greens and let stand 20 minutes. May be chilled up to 24 hours before using. *Makes 1 1/4 cups.*

MEATS

ORANGE SPICED LAMB

2	cloves garlic, crushed	2	teaspoons salt
1	Tablespoon paprika	½	teaspoon pepper
1½	teaspoons dried rosemary	1	6 pound leg of lamb

Sauce

¼	cup butter	¼	cup dry red wine
6	ounces frozen orange juice concentrate		

Preheat oven to 350°. In a small bowl, mix garlic, paprika, rosemary, salt and pepper. Make 12 slits in meat and press part of garlic mixture inside each slit. Bake 18-20 minutes per pound for medium-rare. Make sauce while meat bakes. After meat has baked 1 hour, baste frequently with sauce. When meat is done, remove from oven and let stand 15 minutes before slicing. Serve with remaining sauce. *Serves 10-12.*

To prepare sauce: Place all ingredients in a small saucepan. Simmer 15 minutes, stirring to blend.

Cooking with wine does not necessarily add extra calories . . . 85% of a dry table wine's calories are lost when the heat burns away the alcohol.

MARINATED PORK TENDERLOIN WITH MUSTARD SAUCE

Meat

3	pork tenderloins, each ¾ pound	½	cup Bourbon
½	cup soy sauce	4	Tablespoons brown sugar

Mustard Sauce

½	cup sour cream	1	Tablespoon chopped scallions or onions
½	cup mayonnaise		
1	Tablespoon dry mustard	1½	Tablespoons white wine vinegar

To prepare meat: In a shallow baking dish, blend all ingredients, except meat. Add meat and marinate chilled for several hours. To serve, preheat oven to 325°. Bake meat in marinade 45 minutes, basting frequently. Serve with sauce. *Serves 4.*

To prepare sauce: In a medium bowl, mix all ingredients. Let stand at room temperature at least 4 hours before serving.

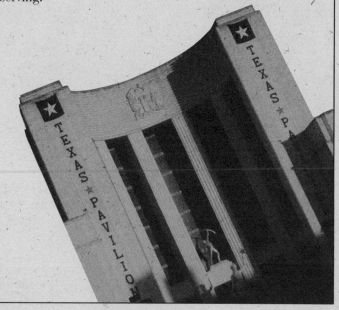

Pork Tenderloin With Red Currant Sauce

½ cup dry sherry
½ cup soy sauce
2 large cloves garlic, minced
1 Tablespoon dry mustard

1 teaspoon ground ginger
1 teaspoon crushed dried thyme
3¾ pound pork tenderloins

Red Currant Sauce

1 10-ounce jar red currant jelly
2 Tablespoons dry sherry

1 Tablespoon soy sauce
¼ cup dried currants (optional)

Combine sherry, soy sauce, garlic, mustard, ginger and thyme in a large ziplock bag and marinate meat at room temperature for 2 hours. Preheat oven to 325°. Bake tenderloins in marinade for 45 minutes or until meat thermometer registers 160-165°. Baste occasionally. Let roast rest 15 minutes before carving. Serve with red currant sauce. *Serves 6.*

Butterflied Leg Of Lamb

2 Tablespoons Dijon mustard
½ teaspoon salt
¼ teaspoon black pepper
4 Tablespoons brown sugar
2 Tablespoons soy sauce

2 Tablespoons olive oil
1 clove garlic, crushed
⅓ cup lemon juice
1 5 pound leg of lamb, butterflied, boned and flattened

Preheat oven to 450°. In a small bowl, combine all ingredients except lamb. Pour over lamb, chill and marinate 4 hours. To serve, drain and reserve sauce. Bake lamb for 35 minutes, basting often with marinade. Remove meat from oven and let stand 10-15 minutes before thinly slicing on the diagonal. (May be cooked on a medium-hot grill 15 minutes per side.) *Serves 8.*

Venison Bourguignon

2 cups dry red wine
1 cup dry sherry
½ cup olive oil
2 teaspoons soy sauce
2 cloves garlic
½ teaspoon thyme
2 bay leaves
dash Tabasco
1 medium onion, thinly sliced
3 pounds venison backstrap or tenderloin, cut into 1½ inch cubes

1 cup flour
salt and pepper
Accent to taste
3 Tablespoons butter, melted
1 cup beef broth
wine or sherry
2 Tablespoons butter, melted
½ pound fresh mushrooms, sliced
2 large carrots, sliced
2 medium onions, thinly sliced

In a large bowl, combine wines, oil, soy sauce, garlic, thyme, bay leaves, Tabasco and onion to make a marinade. Place meat in a glass or stainless steel bowl. Cover with marinade and chill for 12 hours. Drain and pat meat dry, reserving marinade. In a shallow bowl or plastic bag, mix flour, salt, pepper and Accent. Dredge meat a few cubes at a time in flour. In a large, heavy skillet, brown meat in batches in 3 Tablespoons of butter. Strain reserved marinade; add 1 cup to skillet. Return all meat to the skillet, stirring well. Mix in rest of marinade and broth. If there is not enough liquid to cover meat, add wine or sherry. Simmer 1 hour. While meat is simmering, sauté mushrooms in remaining butter in a small skillet until soft. Add mushrooms, carrots and 1 onion to meat. Simmer an additional 2½ hours or until meat is tender. Serve with fresh pasta. *Serves 6-8.*

HUNAN LAMB

¼ cup white wine vinegar
¼ cup hot water
1 pound lamb, sliced in ⅛-inch pieces across grain
½ cup oil
2 green onions (green part), cut in 2-inch slices and slivered

2 cloves garlic, minced
2 cups broccoli flowerettes and peeled sliced stalk
1 cup bok choy (white part), sliced

Marinade

2 Tablespoons peanut oil
2 Tablespoons sherry
2 Tablespoons soy sauce

½ teaspoon ground Szechwan pepper
1½ Tablespoons cornstarch

Sauce

1 Tablespoon Hoisin sauce
1 Tablespoon oyster sauce
2 Tablespoons water

½ Tablespoon sugar
1 Tablespoon sesame oil
1 teaspoon Szechwan chili sauce (or to taste)

In a large bowl, combine lamb, vinegar and hot water. Let rest for 10 minutes. Drain, rinse with cold water and set aside.

To prepare marinade: Heat 2 Tablespoons of peanut oil and transfer to a small bowl. Add sherry, soy sauce, Szechwan pepper and cornstarch. Mix well. Add lamb to marinade and let set for 30 minutes.

To prepare sauce: In a small bowl, combine Hoisin sauce, oyster sauce, water, sugar, sesame oil and chili sauce. Set aside.

To prepare lamb: Drain lamb, reserving marinade. Heat ½ cup oil in a large skillet over high heat. Add green onions and garlic. Cook 1 minute. Add lamb and stir-fry until just done. Remove lamb and onions from skillet with slotted spoon and reserve. Discard all but 2 Tablespoons oil from skillet and add vegetables. Stir-fry briefly, then add reserved lamb, Hoisin Sauce and marinade if too dry. Heat thoroughly. Serves 4.

Cannelloni Escarole

Tomato Sauce

½ cup carrots, finely diced	4 cloves garlic, unpeeled
½ cup onions, finely diced	1 bay leaf
½ cup celery, finely diced	1 teaspoon oregano
6 Tablespoons butter, melted	1 teaspoon basil
2 Tablespoons oil	2-4 Tablespoons tomato paste
4 pounds Italian tomatoes, peeled and chopped	salt

Béchamel Sauce

6 Tablespoons butter	3 cups milk, scalded
4½ Tablespoons flour	salt and white pepper

Filling

1 pound escarole	2 eggs, slightly beaten
2 Tablespoons olive oil	2 Tablespoons whipping cream
¼ cup onions, finely chopped	1 teaspoon oregano
1 clove garlic, finely minced	½ teaspoon basil
1 Tablespoon butter, melted	salt and pepper
1 pound ground chuck	4 12x15-inch fresh pasta sheets
½ cup (3 ounces) mortadella, coarsely chopped	freshly grated Parmesan butter
½ cup grated Parmesan cheese	

To prepare tomato sauce: In a large saucepan, sauté carrots, onions and celery slowly in butter and oil for 10 minutes or until tender but not brown. Stir in tomatoes, garlic and herbs. Simmer 1½-2 hours, adding water if necessary. Remove garlic and discard. Stir in tomato paste and salt. Transfer to a food processor fitted with the metal blade and process in batches until smooth.

To prepare béchamel sauce: In a saucepan, melt butter over low heat. Whisk in flour and cook slowly for 2 minutes; do not brown. Remove from heat and add hot milk all at once, whisking vigorously. Return to heat and stir until thickened. Season to taste.

To prepare filling: Steam escarole 3-4 minutes or until limp. Drain well on paper towels and chop finely. In a large skillet, sauté onion and garlic in oil until soft but not brown. Add escarole and continue to cook, stirring, 4-5 minutes. When almost all moisture is gone, transfer to a large mixing bowl. Set aside. In a skillet, lightly brown chuck in butter. Drain meat and stir into escarole along with mortadella, Parmesan, cream, eggs and spices. Blend well.

To assemble: Cut each pasta sheet into 12 4x5-inch rectangles. Spoon 1 Tablespoon filling into each rectangle. Turn up the ends overlapping to form a tube shape. In a large, flat baking dish, place pasta seam-side down. Layer in the following order; tomato sauce, béchamel sauce and more tomato sauce. Sprinkle with Parmesan and dot with butter. Bake 30 minutes, then broil for 30 seconds to lightly brown. (May be frozen and thawed before baking.) *Serves 10.*

BENGAL CURRY

2	Tablespoons flour	3	Tablespoons brown
1½	teaspoons salt		sugar
2	Tablespoons curry	3	Tablespoons seedless
	powder		raisins
2	pounds lamb, veal or	1	Tablespoon
	chicken, cut into bite-		Worcestershire sauce
	size pieces	3	slices lemon
⅓	cup butter, melted	2	Tablespoons grated
2	large onions, chopped		unsweetened coconut
2	apples, peeled, cored	⅓	cup chopped walnuts
	and chopped	2	cups chicken stock or
1	clove garlic, minced		water

In a shallow dish (or paperbag), mix flour, salt and curry. Toss meat in flour to coat well. Reserve flour. Transfer meat to a large saucepan and brown in butter. Add the onions, apples, garlic, sugar, raisins, Worcestershire, lemon, coconut and nuts and cook 5 minutes. Stir in stock and reserved flour. Bring to a boil. Cover and lower heat. Simmer for several hours, stirring occasionally. Flavor improves with cooking and age so may be made up to 2 days in advance. Discard lemon slices before serving. *Serves 5-6.*

LEMON-HERB PORK CHOPS

¼	cup lemon juice	¼	teaspoon ground thyme
2	Tablespoons vegetable	¼	teaspoon dried oregano
	oil	¼	teaspoon black pepper
3	cloves garlic, minced	6	pork chops, 1-inch
1	teaspoon salt		thick

In a shallow dish, blend all ingredients, except meat. Add pork chops. Cover and chill 12 hours, turning meat occasionally. To serve, remove meat from marinade. Grill over hot coals 15-20 minutes per side or until done, basting chops with marinade. *Serves 6.*

SAUSAGE FILLED CRÊPES WITH DILL SAUCE

Crepes

1	pound bulk hot sausage	3	ounces cream cheese
¼	cup chopped onion	8	crêpes
½	cup grated Cheddar		
	cheese		

Sauce

½	cup sour cream		dill weed to taste
2	Tablespoons butter,		
	softened		

To prepare filling: In a large skillet, cook sausage and onion until meat is browned. Drain. Transfer to a large bowl. Stir in cheeses until well blended. Spoon filling into each crêpe. Roll up crêpes and place in a glass baking dish. Cover and chill. Before serving, preheat oven to 375°. Bake uncovered for 35 minutes. Remove from oven, top with sauce and continue baking 5 more minutes. Serve immediately. *Makes 8 crêpes.* To prepare sauce: In a small bowl, mix all ingredients until blended.

Note: Can be prepared in advance and frozen before baking. Can be halved or doubled.

Delicate sauces such as hollandaise and buerre-blanc can be prepared ahead and held in a thermos. Be sure to run warm water in the thermos and dry thoroughly before pouring sauce in.

Italian Sausage Lasagna

Tomato Sauce

3	Tablespoons olive oil	1	teaspoon oregano
1	pound ground chuck, crumbled		salt and pepper
1	pound Italian sausage, crumbled	3	Tablespoons parsley, chopped
		6	ounces tomato paste
1	medium onion, chopped	2	9-ounce cans tomatoes, coarsely chopped, with juice
1	medium green bell pepper, chopped		
½	pound fresh mushrooms, sliced	2	tomatoes, chopped
3	cloves garlic, minced	1	Tablespoon Italian seasoning
1	teaspoon basil, chopped	1	teaspoon garlic salt

Béchamel Sauce

3	Tablespoons butter	2¼ -2½ cups milk	
3	Tablespoons flour	salt and white pepper	

1	pound lasagna noodles, cooked	3	cups grated Parmesan cheese
1	pound Mozzarella cheese, sliced		

To make tomato sauce: In a large saucepan, heat oil. Add meats and onion and brown, stirring well. Mix in remaining ingredients. Cover and simmer 45 minutes, stirring occasionally.

To make béchamel sauce: In a medium saucepan over low heat, melt butter. Gradually whisk in flour. Slowly add milk, stirring constantly. Season with salt and pepper. Continue to cook over low heat until sauce becomes slightly thickened.

To assemble lasagna: Preheat oven to 375°. In a greased three quart casserole dish layer as follows: thin coating of tomato sauce, noodles, thin coating of béchamel sauce, Mozzarella, Parmesan. Repeat until all ingredients are used. Bake 20 minutes or until bubbly. *Serves 10-12.*

Medallions Of Venison

1½	cups bread crumbs	4	Tablespoons extra virgin olive oil
½	cup grated Parmesan cheese	1	cup beef or game broth
	grated rind of 2 lemons	¼	cup red wine
1	backstrap of antelope, venison or elk	1	green bell pepper, sliced into rings
	Greek seasoning	1	red bell pepper, sliced into rings
½	cup flour		
5	Tablespoons butter		

In a medium bowl, mix crumbs, cheese and rind. Slice backstrap into medallions. Sprinkle medallions with seasoning and dust with flour, shaking off excess. Dredge in the crumb mixture, pressing it firmly into each medallion. In a large skillet, melt butter with oil and brown game, being careful medallions do not stick to the pan. Add broth and wine. Cover game with pepper rings. Cover skillet and simmer 45 minutes. Transfer game to a warm platter. Increase heat to medium-high and reduce sauce 5 minutes, scraping pan frequently. Season to taste. Pour sauce over game. *Serves 6.*

PORK CHOPS WITH APPLES AND SAGE

4	pork chops
2	Tablespoons oil
4	medium onions, finely chopped
1	Tablespoon flour
¾	cup chicken stock
2	large, tart apples, peeled, cored and thickly sliced

1	teaspoon dried sage
¼	teaspoon meat extract
	salt and pepper
	fresh parsley

In a large, heavy skillet, brown chops lightly on both sides in oil. Remove from pan and set aside. In the same pan, sauté onions until lightly golden. Stir in flour, stock, apples, sage and extract. Return chops to pan and simmer 30 minutes or until tender. Season with salt and pepper. Garnish with parsley. *Serves 4.*

SAUSAGE VEAL LOAF

½	cup milk
1	egg, beaten
2	slices French bread, torn into pieces
½	cup bread crumbs
1	pound ground chuck
½	pound ground veal
¼	pound mild Italian sausage
2	stalks celery with leaves, finely chopped

1	onion, chopped
2	cloves garlic, crushed
½	green bell pepper, chopped
2	Tablespoons tomato paste
1	Tablespoon dried Italian seasoning
1	teaspoon tarragon
½	teaspoon seasoned salt

Preheat oven to 325°. In a large bowl, mix milk with egg. Add bread and crumbs. Let soak for a few minutes. Blend in remaining ingredients. Shape into a loaf pan. Bake 1 hour; remove from oven, drain off excess fat and return to oven. Bake 1 additional hour. *Serves 6.*

VEAL WITH RED AND GREEN PEPPERS

4	Tablespoons unsalted butter, melted
2	Tablespoons olive oil
2	large cloves garlic, minced
1	medium onion, thinly sliced
1	medium green bell pepper, thinly sliced
1	medium red bell pepper, thinly sliced
	zest of ½ lemon

¾	pound fresh mushrooms, sliced
12	(2 pounds) large veal scallops, pounded thin
	whole wheat flour
4	Tablespoons unsalted butter, melted
2	Tablespoons olive oil
	salt and pepper
¼	cup fresh lemon juice
6	sprigs fresh parsley, chopped

In a large skillet, sauté garlic, onions, peppers and zest in 4 Tablespoons butter and 2 Tablespoons olive oil for 6-8 minutes. Add mushrooms and cook 2-3 minutes. Remove vegetables from skillet and set aside. Dust veal with flour. In same skillet, add remaining butter and oil and sauté for 1-2 minutes per side. Remove veal to a platter. Season with salt and pepper. Add lemon juice to skillet and deglaze over medium-high heat. Pour over veal. Top with vegetables and sprinkle with parsley. Serve immediately. *Serves 6.*

Steak With Black Peppercorns

½ cup butter, melted
2 large shallots, finely sliced
¼ cup whole black peppercorns
4 10-ounce beef tenderloin fillets

salt
¼ cup Cognac, warmed
2 teaspoons Dijon mustard
¼ cup whipping cream
parsley
fresh strawberries

In a large skillet, sauté shallots in butter. Season fillets with salt. Crush peppercorns with a rolling pin. Press an even coating of peppercorns on both sides of fillets. Grill meat, basting with ½ of the shallot mixture for 10 minutes (rare), 15 minutes (medium) or as desired. Transfer cooked meat to the skillet with remaining shallot mixture. Pour Cognac over meat and flame. Transfer meat to a platter. Stir into shallot mixture the mustard and cream. Heat, blending well. Pour over meat and garnish with parsley and fruit. *Serves 4.*

Veal Scallops With Roquefort

4 ounces Roquefort cheese
½ cup unsalted butter
2 Tablespoons Dijon mustard
2 pinches cayenne pepper
12 veal scallops

⅓ cup flour
4 eggs, slightly beaten
3 cups bread crumbs
14 Tablespoons unsalted butter, melted
oil
lemon wedges

In a food processor fitted with the metal blade, process cheese, ½ cup butter, mustard and pepper until very creamy. Spread mixture on one side of veal. Coat both sides with flour. Dip in egg, then coat with crumbs. Chill 30 minutes. In a large skillet, sauté veal in remaining butter mixed with a little oil to prevent burning. Cook cheese-side last. Garnish with lemon. *Serves 12.*

Steak Adobe

Meat

4 strip steaks
4 slices panela (or desired white Mexican cheese)

Sauce

½ cup chopped onions
1 Tablespoon olive oil
1 fresh jalapeño, seeded
¼ teaspoon dried oregano
½ cup fresh cilantro leaves
1 teaspoon chicken base or instant chicken bouillon

1 small clove garlic
1 teaspoon Worcestershire sauce
½ teaspoon seasoned salt
1 8-ounce can chopped green chilies
2 teaspoons red currant jelly

Grill meat over medium-hot coals 6-8 minutes. Turn over and top with cheese, grilling 5 additional minutes for medium-rare. Remove meat from heat. Top with sauce and serve. *Serves 4.*

To prepare sauce: In a medium-saucepan, sauté onion in oil 3 minutes. Transfer to a food processor fitted with metal blade. Add remaining ingredients and process until well blended. Return mixture to the pan and simmer 10 minutes.

Coriander is the seeds of cilantro — the pungent chinese parsley. Sometimes both terms are used for the herb.

VEAL NICOISE

Sauce

1 Tablespoon butter, melted	2-3 pepperoncini, chopped (small dried red peppers)
1 Tablespoon olive oil	
2 Tablespoons chopped shallots or onions	salt and pepper
1 Tablespoon minced garlic	1 pound fresh tomatoes, peeled and chopped
	2-3 fresh basil leaves

Veal

1 pound veal slices	⅓ cup dry white wine
flour	¾ cup whole black olives, pitted
2-3 Tablespoons butter, melted	
	parsley sprigs

To prepare sauce: In a medium saucepan, heat butter and oil. Sauté shallots and garlic. Add pepperoncini. Stir briskly 1 minute. Mix in tomatoes and basil. Simmer 10 minutes or until slightly reduced.

To prepare veal: Pound veal until ¼-inch thick or less. Dredge in flour, shaking to remove excess. In a large skillet, sauté in butter 1 minute per side. Add wine. Lower heat and simmer 3-5 minutes, turning several times. Do not brown. Transfer veal to simmering sauce. Add olives and simmer 5-7 minutes. Adjust seasonings. To serve, place veal in center of plates. Top with sauce and garnish with parsley. *Serves 4.*

"To receive a guest in one's home is the most complimentary kind of hospitality." Genevieve Antoine Dariaux (Director of Haute Couture House of Nina Ricci)

STEAK WITH BLEU CHEESE BUTTER

Bleu Cheese Butter

5-6 Tablespoons butter	chopped fresh parsley
½-¾ cup bleu cheese	3 cloves garlic, pressed
5-6 green onions, chopped	
1 2½ -3-inch thick sirloin steak	

To prepare butter: In a small bowl or a food processor fitted with the metal blade, combine all ingredients until well blended.

To prepare steak: Grill steak. Three or four minutes before desired doneness is reached, place butter mixture on top. Finish grilling, letting the cheese melt but not run down the sides. Slice diagonally across the grain to serve. *Serves 6.*

VEAL CHOPS PORCINI

1 ounce porcini mushrooms, chopped	2-3 Tablespoons butter, melted
⅓ cup warm water	½ cup dry white wine
4 veal chops	1 cup beef broth
flour	juice of ½ lemon
salt and pepper	

Soak mushrooms in water for 20 minutes to reconstitute. Drain if necessary and set aside. Lightly flour chops, season with salt and pepper and brown in butter in a large skillet over medium-high heat. Remove to a platter. Add wine to skillet. Deglaze and reduce until ½ of the liquid remains. Stir in broth and reduce until ½ of liquid remains. Add mushrooms and chops to skillet. Pour lemon juice over all. Cover, reduce heat to low and simmer 10-15 minutes. *Serves 4.*

VEAL-ARTICHOKE TART

Pastry

1¾	cups flour	1	cup ricotta cheese
½	cup butter	½	teaspoon salt

Filling

¼	pound ground veal	14	ounces artichoke hearts
¼	pound ground fresh		(not marinated),
	pork		drained
3	Tablespoons olive oil	¾	cup ricotta cheese
1	small onion, finely	2	eggs, beaten
	chopped	1	Tablespoon fresh
1	medium carrot, finely		parsley, finely snipped
	chopped		salt and pepper
1	rib celery, finely	½	cup freshly grated
	chopped		Parmesan cheese
1	clove garlic, minced		

To prepare pastry: In a large bowl, blend all ingredients with a pastry blender until mixture resembles pea-size pieces. Cover and chill.

To prepare filling: Blend together meats. Set aside. In a large skillet, sauté onion, carrot, celery and garlic in oil. Add meats and cook 10 minutes. Cool. Chop artichokes and add to meat mixture along with remaining ingredients. Blend well.

To assemble: Preheat oven to 375°. Divide and roll out dough as for a double crust pie. Fit half of dough into a deep dish pie plate. Fill with meat mixture and top with remaining crust. Cut vents in top crust and bake 45 minutes. Cool 10-15 minutes before slicing. *Serves 6.*

Never cover the pan while boiling green vegetables. They will not stay green and may turn grey.

MARINADE FOR WILD GAME

2	onions, thinly sliced	¼	cup Worcestershire
2	carrots, coarsely		sauce
	chopped	2	teaspoons Tabasco
2	large stalks celery,	2	teaspoons thyme
	coarsely chopped	1	teaspoon marjoram
4	cloves garlic, crushed	1	teaspoon oregano
2½	cups burgundy wine		pepper
	juice of 4 limes		
½	cup extra-virgin olive		
	oil		

In a stainless steel or enameled saucepan, blend all ingredients. Bring to a boil. Lower heat and simmer 5 minutes. Remove from heat and cool slightly. Pour over game (2 backstraps or 1 large roast of venison, antelope or elk) and marinate chilled at least 12 hours, turning several times.

SAUSAGE PUFF

2	eggs	¾	pound Italian sausage
½	teaspoon salt		in casing
1	cup flour	2	Tablespoons butter
1	cup milk		
2	Tablespoons chopped		
	parsley		

Preheat oven to 450°. In a large bowl, beat eggs and salt until frothy. Add milk and flour alternately until smooth. Add parsley. Let batter rest at least one hour, covered with plastic wrap. In a large skillet, brown sausage cut into ½ inch pieces. Drain well and set aside. In a large baking dish, melt butter in the preheated oven until the dish is very hot and the butter sizzles. Pour batter into hot dish and sprinkle with the sausage. Bake 15 minutes. Reduce oven to 375° and bake an additional 10 minutes. *Serves 10.*

POULTRY

POLLO SANGRÍA

1½ cups red wine
¾ cup orange juice
3 Tablespoons chili powder
⅓ cup green chilies, chopped
3 Tablespoons olive oil
1 large onion, chopped
3 cloves garlic, minced
1½ teaspoons oregano
2 teaspoons ground cumin
1½ Tablespoons brown sugar
1 bay leaf
grated rind of 1½ oranges
salt
6 pounds chicken, cut in serving pieces.

To prepare marinade: Combine all ingredients except the chicken. Marinate overnight. To prepare chicken: Preheat oven to 350°. In a large shallow pan, arrange chicken pieces and bake for 1 hour, basting frequently with marinade. *Serves 6.*

SCALLOPINI OF TURKEY WITH MOREL AND COGNAC SAUCE

4½ pounds of turkey breast cut into 12 scallopini, about 6 ounces each, pounded until about ⅜-inch thick
4 ounces dried morels, soaked in 4 cups lukewarm water for 1 hour
¾ stick butter
1½ teaspoons seasoned salt
1 teaspoon freshly ground black pepper
½ cup chopped shallots
1 Tablespoon chopped garlic
2 Tablespoons cognac
1½ cups cream
salt and pepper
1 teaspoon potato starch dissolved in 1 Tablespoon water

Drain the morels and remove any dirty or sandy stems. Cut the morels into halves. Strain the juice through paper towels and reduce to 1 cup.

At serving time, use 2 large saucepans or 3 skillets. Divide the butter between the skillets. When hot, add the scallopini. Sprinkle with salt and pepper. Cook over medium to high heat for approximately 1 minute on each side. Arrange in a dish and set in a 180° oven to keep warm.

Add the shallots and garlic to the skillets and sauté 30 seconds. Add the cognac and flambé. Add the reduced mushroom juice and cream. Bring to a boil, stirring to mix any solidified juices. Add the juice which has been released from the scallopini. Strain into a clean saucepan and add the morels. Bring to a boil and simmer for 3 minutes. Add salt and pepper to taste and the dissolved potato starch if the mixture needs thickening. Add a few drops of lemon juice. Arrange the scallopini on a platter or 6 individual plates and coat with the sauce and mushrooms. Serve immediately. *Serves 6-12.*

CHICKEN TETRAZZINI

Chicken

1 5-pound hen
2 carrots, peeled
2 stalks celery
1 medium onion
1 teaspoon salt

Pasta

5 Tablespoons butter, melted
1 Tablespoon fresh lemon juice
1 pound fresh mushrooms, sliced
½ teaspoon salt
1 pound pasta, cooked

Sauce

3 Tablespoons butter, melted
2 Tablespoons flour
½ teaspoon paprika
1½ teaspoons salt
pinch of nutmeg
2 cups reserved chicken broth
¼ cup sherry
1 cup whipping cream
grated fresh Parmesan cheese

To prepare chicken: In a large pot, place all ingredients. Cover with water. Bring to a boil. Reduce heat and simmer 1 hour or until hen is tender. Remove hen, reserving broth. When hen is cool enough to handle, remove and cut meat into bite-size pieces.

To prepare pasta: In a large skillet, sauté mushrooms, lemon juice and salt in butter until mushrooms are tender. Toss with pasta and arrange in a large baking dish.

To prepare sauce: In a large saucepan, whisk butter and flour. Blend in paprika, salt and nutmeg. Cook 20 seconds to prevent lumping. Whisk in reserved broth and sherry. Simmer until thickened. Stir in cream.

To assemble: Preheat oven to 350°. Place chicken pieces over pasta. Cover with sauce. Top with Parmesan. Bake 25-30 minutes. *Serves 10.*

TARRAGON CHICKEN WITH MUSTARD SAUCE

2 Tablespoons butter
1 Tablespoon oil
6 boneless, skinned chicken breast halves
1 Tablespoon butter
1 Tablespoon oil
3 large shallots, minced
½ cup white wine
1 cup chicken stock
2 garlic cloves, minced
¾ cup whipping cream
3 Tablespoons whole grain mustard
1 teaspoon dried tarragon
white pepper to taste
chopped parsley

In a large skillet, sauté chicken in 2 Tablespoons butter and 1 Tablespoon oil over medium-high heat. When lightly browned on both sides, remove and keep warm. Add remaining butter and oil. Sauté shallots until tender. Stir in wine, stock and garlic. Bring to a boil. Continue cooking until ½ cup liquid remains, about 15 minutes. Stir in cream and mustard. Bring to a boil. Cook until slightly thickened. Mix in tarragon and pepper. Return chicken to pan. Cook until tender and hot. To serve, garnish with parsley. *Serves 4-6.*

CHICKEN WITH CHUTNEY

4 whole chicken breasts, halved, boned and skinned
1 cup mayonnaise
1 cup sour cream
¼ cup chutney
2 teaspoons curry powder
2 lemons
freshly ground black pepper

Preheat oven to 450°. In a small bowl, combine mayonnaise and sour cream. Stir in curry and the juice of 2 lemons. Arrange chicken in glass baking dish and cover with sauce, chutney and pepper. Bake for 12 minutes. Serve hot. *Serves 8.*

Note: This exotic dish is wonderful served with couscous.

ROLLED CHICKEN BREASTS WITH FRESH TOMATO SAUCE

Tomato Sauce

2	cups chopped tomatoes
½	cup chopped onions
1	clove garlic, minced
¼	teaspoon oregano
⅛	teaspoon pepper
1	6-ounce can tomato paste

Chicken

4	boneless chicken breast halves
	salt and pepper
	Dijon mustard
	Italian herbs
4	thin slices Mozzarella cheese
	flour
2	Tablespoons olive oil

To prepare sauce: In a medium saucepan, cook tomatoes over medium heat until juices begin to run, about 15 minutes. Stir in onion, garlic, oregano and pepper. Cover and simmer over low heat 15 more minutes. Blend in tomato paste.

To prepare chicken: Preheat oven to 350°. Flatten chicken and sprinkle with salt and pepper. Spread with mustard and sprinkle with herbs. Top with cheese. Roll up each piece using a toothpick to secure. Coat with flour. Brown in a large skillet in oil. Transfer to a large greased casserole dish. Top with sauce. Cover and bake 30 minutes. *Serves 4.*

CHICKEN CHAUDFROID

8	boneless chicken breast halves	¼	teaspoon salt
4	cups chicken broth	2	Tablespoons snipped dill
3	ounces cream cheese, softened	8	very thick slices tomato
4	Tablespoons mayonnaise		romaine lettuce leaves
2	Tablespoons fresh lemon juice		seasoned salt
½	teaspoon grated lemon peel		slivered almonds, toasted
			snipped fresh dill
			avocado slices

In a large pot, bring chicken and broth to a boil. Cover and lower heat to simmer. Cook 30 minutes or until tender. Chill chicken in broth until cool. When ready to serve, blend cheese, mayonnaise, lemon juice, peel, salt and dill to form a paste. Remove chicken from broth and skin. Coat rounded side of chicken with paste. On serving plates layer in the following order on a bed of lettuce, 1 tomato slice, seasoned salt, chicken, almonds and dill. Garnish with avocado. *Serves 8.*

CHICKEN WITH CHILI SAUCE AND CREAM

8	boneless, skinned chicken breast halves	½	teaspoon salt
½	cup chili sauce	1	cup whipping cream
1	teaspoon curry powder	1	pound spinach
¼	teaspoon pepper		linguini, cooked

Make ½-inch slashes on chicken pieces. Place in a deep, buttered baking dish. In a small bowl, mix chili sauce, curry, salt and pepper. Spread over chicken. Cover and chill 2 hours. To serve, preheat oven to 375°. Bake chicken for 15 minutes. Cover with cream and bake 20 more minutes. Serve with hot pasta. *Serves 6-8.*

SESAME CHICKEN WITH PLUM SAUCE

Chicken

12	boneless, skinned chicken breast halves	1	Tablespoon Greek seasoning
1½	cups buttermilk	1	teaspoon salt
2	Tablespoons lemon juice	1	teaspoon pepper
2	teaspoons Worcestershire sauce	2	cloves garlic, minced
		2-3	cups soft bread crumbs
1	teaspoon soy sauce	2-3	cups sesame seeds
1	teaspoon paprika		shortening

Plum Sauce

1½	cups plum jelly	1½	Tablespoons prepared horseradish
1½	Tablespoons Dijon mustard	1½	teaspoons lemon juice

To prepare chicken: Cut each chicken breast into ½-inch strips (5-6 strips per breast). Place in a large shallow pan. In a medium bowl, mix buttermilk, lemon juice, Worcestershire, soy sauce, paprika, seasoning, salt, pepper and garlic. Pour over chicken to cover completely. Marinate 12 hours. When ready to serve, drain chicken. Combine crumbs and sesame seeds. Toss chicken in crumb mixture and deep fat fry at 350°. Drain. Serve with sauce. *Serves 12.*

To prepare sauce: In a small saucepan, mix all ingredients. Warm over low heat.

"The discovery of a new food adds more to human happiness than the discovery of a new star."

POLLO TONNATO

8	boneless chicken breast halves	1¼	cups mayonnaise
½	cup coarsely chopped carrots	⅓	cup finely chopped basil leaves
½	cup coarsely chopped onions	3½	ounces tuna fish packed in oil (do not drain)
½	cup coarsely chopped celery	2	large tomatoes, peeled and cored
½	cup dry white wine		salt and pepper
1	clove garlic, peeled	2	teaspoons extra-virgin olive oil
7	cups water		
	salt	2	Tablespoons drained capers
1	bay leaf		fresh parsley, cilantro or basil leaves
1	teaspoon dried thyme		
6	peppercorns		
6	sprigs fresh parsley		

In a large pot, place chicken, carrots, onions, celery, wine, garlic, water, salt, bay leaf, thyme, peppercorns and parsley. Bring to a boil. Cover and lower heat to simmer. Simmer 15 minutes or until chicken is tender. Remove chicken and set aside to cool, reserving broth. Place 1½ cups broth in a saucepan. Boil over high heat until liquid is reduced to ½ cup. Cool slightly, pour into blender or food processor and add tuna and process until a fine paste forms. Transfer mixture to a large bowl. Blend in mayonnaise and basil. Set aside. Cut tomatoes into thin strips. Place in a bowl and sprinkle with salt, pepper and oil. Toss in capers. To serve, arrange chicken on a platter. Spoon tomatoes around chicken. Nap chicken with one-half of mayonnaise mixture. Garnish with fresh herbs. Serve with remaining mayonnaise. *Serves 4-6.*

ROASTED CORNISH GAME HENS WITH ORANGE GLAZE AND SAUCE

Orange Glaze
1   12-ounce jar orange marmalade
¼   cup Galliano
½   teaspoon whole cloves

Orange Sauce
1   cup chicken broth
1½ teaspoons dried thyme
1   bay leaf
1½ cups orange juice
2   Tablespoons cornstarch
⅓   cup Galliano

Hens
2   6-ounce packages white and wild rice mix
1   cup chopped walnuts
2   teaspoons orange peel
1   cup chopped celery
¼   cup butter, melted
½   cup chopped fresh parsley
salt and black pepper
8   1-pound Cornish game hens

To prepare glaze: In a medium saucepan, mix all ingredients. Heat and keep warm while basting hens.

To prepare hens: Preheat oven to 400°. Cook rice according to package instructions. Blend into cooked rice the nuts, celery, peel, butter and parsley. Salt and pepper hens inside and out. Fill cavity of hens with rice. Secure opening with toothpicks. Truss and cover ends of drumsticks with foil to prevent burning. Place in a roasting pan. Bake 1 hour, basting every 15 minutes with glaze. While hens are baking, make sauce. Serve immediately with sauce. *Serves 8.*

To prepare sauce: In a medium saucepan, mix broth, herbs and juice. Simmer 5 minutes. Take from heat and remove bay leaf. Measure 1 cup of sauce and mix well with cornstarch. Return thickened mixture to remaining sauce in pan. Stir well and cook until thickened. Whisk in liqueur. Serve warm.

CHICKEN NUGGETS WITH LEMON CREAM SAUCE

Lemon Cream Sauce
4   Tablespoons butter, melted
4   Tablespoons flour
salt and pepper
¼   teaspoon paprika
2   teaspoons chicken bouillon granules
1½ cups water
1   cup whipping cream
2   teaspoons lemon juice

Chicken
½   cup flour
1   teaspoon salt
1   teaspoon paprika
3   large whole boneless, skinned chicken breasts
½   cup milk
oil
4   cups hot cooked rice
parsley or lemon slices

To prepare sauce: In a medium saucepan, whisk butter, flour, salt, pepper and bouillon. Gradually whisk in water. Cook, stirring constantly, until boiling and thick. Stir in cream and heat thoroughly. To serve, blend in lemon juice.

To prepare chicken: In a small bowl, mix flour, salt and paprika. Cut chicken into bite-size pieces (or ½-inch long strips). Dip pieces in milk and roll in the flour mixture. Fry in oil until brown. Keep warm. When ready to serve, layer chicken on a bed of rice. Cover with sauce. Garnish with parsley or lemon slices. *Serves 4-6.*

Fresh chicken should have white not yellow skin and not have excess moisture.

CRUNCHY CHICKEN CASSEROLE

2½ cups cooked bite-size chicken pieces	1 teaspoon salt
1 cup chopped celery	3 Tablespoons lemon juice
¼ cup chopped green bell pepper	3 Tablespoons grated onion
½ cup fresh sliced mushrooms	1 cup mayonnaise
1 2-ounce jar pimientos	1 cup grated sharp cheese
½ cup slivered almonds, toasted	1½ cups finely crushed potato chips
1 teaspoon Accent	grated Parmesan cheese
½ teaspoon black pepper	

Preheat oven to 350°. In a 2-quart casserole dish, mix chicken, celery, green pepper, mushrooms, pimientos, nuts, seasonings, lemon juice, onion and mayonnaise. In the following order, layer sharp cheese, chips and Parmesan. Cover and bake 35 minutes. Uncover and brown 5-7 more minutes. *Serves 6.*

CHICKEN À L'ORANGE

flour	1 clove garlic, minced
4-6 large boneless, skinned chicken breast halves	juice of 1 lemon
salt and lemon pepper	½ cup orange marmalade
paprika to taste	½ cup chicken broth
¼ cup butter, melted	1 teaspoon brown sugar
1 medium onion, chopped	⅛ teaspoon nutmeg
	⅛ teaspoon cinnamon

Sprinkle chicken with flour, salt, pepper and paprika. Place in a large skillet and sauté in butter, browning on all sides. Remove chicken. Drain off fat, reserving 3 Tablespoons. Add onion and garlic and sauté until tender. Stir in remaining ingredients. Cook, stirring until marmalade melts. Return chicken to skillet. Simmer uncovered over low heat, 20-30 minutes or until tender, spooning sauce over chicken occasionally. *Serves 4-6.*

CHICKEN BREASTS WITH MUSHROOM MARSALA WINE SAUCE

4 boneless, skinned chicken breast halves	flour
	salt and pepper
1 cup whipping cream	½ cup butter, melted
5 large mushrooms, sliced	½ cup dry Marsala wine
2 Tablespoons butter, melted	

Place chicken in cream for 1 hour at room temperature (or up to 4 hours in refrigerator). In a small skillet, sauté mushrooms in butter. Set aside. When ready to serve, remove chicken from cream, reserving cream. Lightly coat chicken with flour and season with salt and pepper. In a large skillet, brown chicken in remaining butter, turning once. Add mushrooms and wine. Reduce heat to low. In a small saucepan, heat cream and add to chicken. Cover and simmer 15 minutes or until chicken is tender. *Serves 3-4.*

CHICKEN BREASTS WITH PASTA AND OLIVES

¼	cup olive oil	1	8¼-ounce can whole tomatoes, liquid reserved
1	medium onion, chopped		
2	cloves garlic, minced		
1	teaspoon salt	3	mushrooms, sliced
1	teaspoon tumeric	½	cup sliced black olives
1	teaspoon cumin	½	cup dry white wine
¼	teaspoon cayenne pepper	2	Tablespoons cornstarch
4	boneless, skinned chicken breast halves		cooked spaghettini or angel hair pasta

In a large skillet, heat oil over medium-high heat. Add onion and garlic. Sauté 3 minutes. Add salt, tumeric, cumin and cayenne. Add chicken and cook until light golden, about 3 minutes per side. Cut tomatoes into quarters. Add tomatoes and liquid to chicken. Add mushrooms, olives and wine. Reduce heat to low. Cover and cook until chicken is tender, about 15 minutes. Remove chicken and keep warm. Mix cornstarch with a little water, and whisk it into the sauce. Cook until thickened. Cut chicken into bite-sized pieces and return chicken to sauce. Serve over hot pasta. *Serves 4.*

"The creator obliged man to eat in order to live, inviting him to do so by giving him an appetite and rewarding him with pleasure."

OLIVE CHICKEN WITH SAFFRON RICE

Rice

1½	cups water
⅔	cup long-grained rice
½	teaspoon salt
⅓	teaspoon saffron
½	cup fresh lemon juice

Chicken

3	Tablespoons flour	1½	teaspoons fresh lemon juice
	dash paprika		
4	boneless, skinned chicken breast halves	¾	cup pimiento-stuffed green olives
½	cup butter, melted	½	pound fresh mushrooms, sliced
1	large onion, chopped		
1	clove garlic, pressed	1	15-ounce can artichoke hearts, drained
⅔	cup sherry		
1	cup water	2	Tablespoons water
2	cubes chicken bouillon	1	Tablespoon flour
1¼	teaspoons basil		
	dash black pepper		

To prepare rice: In a large saucepan, bring water to a boil. Add remaining ingredients. Cover and reduce heat. Simmer until tender, 30 minutes.

To prepare chicken: While rice is cooking, combine flour and paprika and coat chicken. In a large skillet, brown chicken in butter. Remove and reserve chicken. In same skillet, sauté onion and garlic. Add sherry, water, bouillon, basil, pepper and lemon juice. Bring to a boil. Reduce to simmer. Add olives, mushrooms, artichokes and chicken. Cover and simmer 25 minutes. Transfer chicken to a platter. In remaining broth, stir in water and flour. Cook until smooth and thickened. Pour over chicken. Serve with hot rice. *Serves 4.*

SANTA FE CHICKEN

2	Tablespoons butter	2	cloves garlic, minced
3	whole boneless,	1	Tablespoon flour
	skinned chicken breasts	¾	cup chicken broth
1	teaspoon salt	½	cup plain yogurt or
¼	teaspoon pepper		sour cream
½	pound fresh	½	cup grated Monterey
	mushrooms, sliced		Jack cheese
¼	cup chicken broth	¼	cup pine nuts, toasted
1	Tablespoon butter		
1	onion, chopped		
1	4-ounce can diced		
	green chilies, drained		
	and seeded		

Preheat oven to 350°. In a large skillet, melt butter. Add chicken. Cook, turning as needed, for 10 minutes or until brown on both sides. Season with salt and pepper. Arrange chicken in a single layer in a 9x13-inch glass baking dish. Add mushrooms to the skillet and sauté 3 minutes. Scatter mushrooms over chicken and pour broth over all. Cover and bake 15 minutes.

Melt remaining butter in skillet and sauté onion for 3 minutes. Add chilies, garlic and flour. Cook for 1 minute, stirring constantly. Remove chicken from oven. Combine pan drippings and remaining broth in a measuring cup. Measure 1 cup and stir into onion mixture. Mix in yogurt and heat thoroughly. Spoon mixture over chicken. Sprinkle with cheese and return to oven. Bake for 15 more minutes. To serve, sprinkle with nuts. *Serves 4.*

To test if chicken is done, prick meaty part of the thigh with a fork. The juices should run clear.

CHICKEN FLORENTINE

2	Tablespoons butter	2	cups diced cooked
3	Tablespoons flour		chicken
1	teaspoon salt	1	10-ounce package
dash cayenne pepper			frozen spinach, cooked
½	teaspoon dry mustard		and drained well
2	cups milk	1	Tablespoon butter,
⅓	cup shredded		melted
	Parmesan cheese	⅓	cup fine cracker
½	cup half-and-half		crumbs
	cream		

Preheat oven to 350°. In a medium saucepan, melt 2 Tablespoons butter. Blend in flour, salt, cayenne and mustard. Whisk in milk. Cook over medium heat until thick. Add cheese, cream and chicken, stirring until cheese melts. In a shallow 1½-quart casserole dish, spread spinach and cover with chicken mixture. Combine remaining butter and crumbs. Sprinkle over chicken. Bake 20 minutes. *Serves 4-6.*

CHICKEN BREASTS WITH FRESH MOZZARELLA

4	boneless, skinned	¼	cup white wine
	chicken breast halves,	½	pound fresh
	butterflied		Mozzarella, sliced
2	cups chopped fresh	2	sprigs fresh tarragon,
	mushrooms		chopped
2	Tablespoons butter,		salt and pepper
	melted		

In a large skillet, sauté chicken and mushrooms in butter until golden brown. Add wine and simmer for a few seconds. Top each chicken breast with cheese and sprinkle with tarragon. Cover pan and remove from heat. Remove cover when cheese has melted. Season with salt and pepper. Serve immediately. *Serves 4.*

CHICKEN STRUDEL WITH BÉCHAMEL SAUCE

Strudel

1½ cups chopped celery
1 cup chopped onions
1½ Tablespoons butter, melted
3 cups chopped cooked chicken
3 Tablespoons chicken broth
3 Tablespoons parsley, chopped
½ teaspoon salt
⅛ teaspoon pepper
1 egg, beaten
6 Tablespoons butter, melted
12 phyllo sheets
parsley, chopped

Béchamel Sauce

3 Tablespoons butter, melted
¼ cup finely chopped onions
3 Tablespoons flour
2 cups scalded milk or half-and-half cream
dash white pepper
2 Tablespoons fresh basil

To prepare strudel: Preheat oven to 350°. In a large saucepan, sauté onion and celery in butter until soft. Mix in chicken and broth. Cook until broth is absorbed. Add spices. Remove from heat. Stir in egg and set aside. Prepare phyllo according to package instructions. Using 6 sheets, brush each with butter and stack. Spoon one-half of chicken mixture on top of stack, leaving 1-inch rim around the edge. Turn 1 end up over chicken and fold sides over. Roll up like a jelly roll (widthwise). Place in a greased shallow baking dish, seam-side down. Repeat procedure with remaining 6 sheets. Brush tops with butter. Cut 3 or 4 slits in tops. Bake 40 minutes or until brown and crisp. While baking, make sauce. To serve, slice strudel. Spoon sauce over strudel and sprinkle with parsley. *Serves 6-8.*

To prepare sauce: In a medium saucepan, sauté onion in butter over low heat until soft but not brown. Whisk in flour. Cook 2-3 minutes, whisking constantly. Remove from heat and whisk in hot milk until smooth. Return to medium-low heat. Add pepper and basil. Simmer 10 minutes, stirring occasionally. If too thick, thin with a little warmed chicken broth until desired consistency is reached.

CHICKEN GOURMANDISE

3 cups fresh bread crumbs
1 cup ground almonds
4 teaspoons oil
2 eggs
2 teaspoons water
4 ounces walnut gourmandise cheese
1 Tablespoon dried oregano (thyme or tarragon)
8 boneless, skinned chicken breast halves
3 Tablespoons flour
¾ cup unsalted clarified butter

In a large flat dish, mix crumbs and almonds. In a small bowl, blend oil, eggs and water. Divide cheese into 8 oval-shaped pieces (about 1½ teaspoons each). Roll cheese in oregano. With a very sharp knife, make a small pocket in the thickest part of each chicken breast. Stuff each pocket with a piece of the cheese. Dust chicken with a little flour. Dip in the egg mixture and coat heavily with the crumb mixture. Chill at least 2 hours. When ready to serve, in a large skillet sauté chicken in butter until golden, turning once or 3-4 minutes per side. *Serves 4.*

CASHEW CHICKEN

6	boneless, skinned chicken breast halves	2	packages frozen Chinese pea pods
¼	cup soy sauce	½	pound fresh mushrooms, sliced
2	Tablespoons cornstarch	1	cup chicken stock
½	teaspoon sugar	1	8-ounce can water chestnuts, drained
½	teaspoon salt		
1	Tablespoon oil	4	green onions, sliced
4	ounces cashew nuts		hot cooked rice
3	Tablespoons oil		

Cut chicken into bite-size pieces. In a small bowl, mix soy sauce, cornstarch, sugar and salt until well blended. In an electric skillet (350°) or a large heavy skillet, heat 1 Tablespoon oil. Add nuts and cook 1 minute until brown. Remove nuts and set aside. Add remaining oil. Heat oil and add chicken. Cook until chicken turns opaque. Stir in peas, mushrooms and stock. Cover and simmer 2 minutes. Add chestnuts and soy sauce mixture. Cover and cook until sauce is thick. Uncover and cook 1 minute. Mix in onions and sprinkle with nuts. Serve with hot rice. *Serves 4-6.*

PHEASANT IN TOMATO HERB SAUCE

1	large pheasant
	salt and pepper
1	cup water
1½	cups sherry

Tomato Herb Sauce

1	green bell pepper, finely chopped	1	teaspoon dry mustard
3	stalks celery, finely chopped	2	Tablespoons steak sauce
1	medium onion, finely chopped	2	Tablespoons Worcestershire sauce
½	cup water	½	teaspoon paprika
1	cup butter	⅛	cup apple cider vinegar
2	6-ounce cans tomato paste	1	cup water
1	teaspoon salt	1	bay leaf, crushed
1	teaspoon pepper	5	dashes Tabasco
		2	teaspoons sugar

To prepare pheasant: Cut bird in half, lengthwise. Season with salt and pepper. Cook bird covered in a dutch oven on top of the stove with enough water (about 1 cup of water) to steam bird one hour. While bird is cooking, prepare sauce. Drain grease from steamed pheasant, add sauce and continue cooking uncovered for 30 minutes. Add sherry and simmer 20 more minutes. *Serves 2-3.*

To prepare sauce: In a 2-quart saucepan, place pepper, celery, onion and ½ cup water. Simmer 30 minutes uncovered. Stir in remaining ingredients and simmer an additional 30 minutes.

Note: For a variation, substitute 2 wild ducks for the pheasant.

FISH AND SHELLFISH

SHRIMP AND CRAB MEAT ROMANOFF

6   cups hot cooked rice
½   cup chopped chives
2   cups cottage cheese
8 ounces sliced mushrooms
1   cup sour cream
1   cup mayonnaise
1½ teaspoons salt
½   teaspoon black pepper
½   teaspoon cayenne
    pepper
2   teaspoons
    Worcestershire sauce
¼   cup grated Parmesan
    cheese
dash Tabasco
1½ pounds cooked shrimp,
    peeled
½   pound lump crab meat
paprika
¼   cup grated Parmesan
    cheese for topping

Preheat oven to 350°. In a large bowl, mix together all ingredients except shrimp, crab and paprika until well blended. Stir in shrimp and crab. Spoon into greased 3-quart casserole dish. Sprinkle with paprika and cheese. Bake 30 minutes until hot and bubbly. *Serves 10.*

CRAB, MUSHROOM AND CHEESE TART

Pastry for one 10-inch pie
    shell
1   cup sliced fresh
    mushrooms
1   teaspoon butter, melted
1   pound fresh white crab
    meat (lump or flaked)
1⅓ cups finely diced
    Gruyère or Swiss cheese
¾   cup sour cream
¼   cup mayonnaise
½   teaspoon salt
1   teaspoon flour
1   cup half-and-half
    cream
3   eggs, lightly beaten
½   teaspoon Tabasco

Preheat oven to 450°. Roll out pastry and fit into 10-inch pie plate. Weight with beans or rice; bake 10 minutes. Remove from oven and discard weights. Set shell aside. In a small skillet, sauté mushrooms in butter for 2 minutes. In the following order scatter mushrooms, crab and cheese in partially baked pie shell. Mix sour cream, mayonnaise, salt, flour and cream. Blend in eggs and Tabasco. Pour into shell. Reduce oven to 350° and bake 55 minutes or until set. Remove from oven and let stand 15 minutes before cutting. *Serves 6.*

Note: If crust begins to brown too much, cover loosely with foil.

NEW ENGLAND HOT CRAB MEAT SANDWICHES

½   pound crab meat
1   Tablespoon lemon juice
½   cup mayonnaise
1   small onion, minced
1½ cups diced Swiss
    cheese
1¼ cups sliced ripe olives
salt and pepper
6   round French rolls
butter

Preheat oven to 325°. In a medium bowl, combine all ingredients except bread and butter. Set aside. Slice top off rolls. Scoop out part of the soft centers from the bottom of each roll to form a shell. Butter inside of shells. Spoon crab mixture into shells. Replace with top. Wrap rolls in foil and bake 20-25 minutes. Serve immediately. *Serves 4-6.*

STUFFED CRABS

4½ Tablespoons butter, melted
½ large onion, chopped
½ green bell pepper, chopped
½ cup chopped celery
6 Tablespoons flour
1½ cups milk
salt and pepper
Tabasco

Worcestershire sauce
garlic powder
1 pound lump crab meat
2 hard-boiled eggs, chopped
2 Tablespoons parsley, chopped
¾ cup dry bread crumbs (approximately)
butter

Preheat oven to 325°. In a large saucepan, sauté onion, pepper and celery in butter until soft. Stir in flour until smooth. Slowly add milk, stirring constantly until thick and smooth. Remove from heat. Season generously with salt, pepper, Tabasco, Worcestershire and garlic powder. Mix in crab, eggs and parsley, stirring carefully so as not to shred crab. Fold in enough crumbs to hold mixture together (do not make it too dry). Spoon into buttered scallop shells or ramekins. Top with additional crumbs and dot with butter. Bake 30 minutes. *Serves 8.*

SCALLOPS IN WINE SAUCE

2 pounds bay or sea scallops
4 sprigs celery leaves
1 teaspoon onion salt
1½ cups dry vermouth
¼ cup onion, chopped
½ pound mushrooms, thinly sliced
1 Tablespoon parsley, chopped
½ cup water

8 Tablespoons butter
5 Tablespoons flour
3 egg yolks, beaten
½ cup milk
2 Tablespoons lemon juice
½ teaspoon pepper
2 Tablespoons butter
6 Tablespoons fresh bread crumbs

Preheat oven to 400°. In a large saucepan, simmer scallops, celery leaves and onion salt in vermouth for 2 minutes. Remove scallops to a bowl with a slotted spoon, discard the celery leaves and reserve vermouth. In a medium saucepan, simmer onions, mushrooms and parsley in water for 5 minutes until tender. Set aside. In another large saucepan, melt 8 Tablespoons of butter. Whisk in flour, blending until smooth. Add reserved vermouth slowly, continuing to whisk until smooth. Add onion-mushroom mixture and stir until sauce is smooth and thick. Combine the egg yolks with the milk and add to the sauce, stirring constantly. Do not let mixture boil. Blend in lemon juice and pepper. Add scallops. Spoon mixture into 6 lightly buttered ramekins. In a small skillet, melt 2 Tablespoons butter and toss breadcrumbs to coat. Sprinkle bread crumbs over each ramekin and bake for 10 minutes, or until tops are browned. *Serves 8.*

"Tradition is the handicap by means of which yesterday keeps up with today."

GRILLED SWORDFISH

Marinade

½	cup soy sauce	2	Tablespoons lemon juice
¼	cup tomato sauce or catsup	1	teaspoon pepper
¼	cup parsley, chopped	2	pounds 1-inch thick swordfish
½	cup orange juice		
2	cloves garlic, crushed		

To prepare marinade: In a medium bowl, combine all ingredients until well blended.

To prepare fish: In a shallow dish, pour marinade over fish. Marinate 2-4 hours. Remove fish from marinade and grill fish over hot coals for 8 minutes. Turn and grill 6-8 more minutes, being careful not to overcook. Baste frequently with reserved marinade. Serve immediately. *Serves 4.*

FILLET OF RED SNAPPER IN RED WINE SAUCE

Red Wine Sauce

2-3 Tablespoons finely chopped shallots	fresh lemon juice
1 cup dry red wine	5-6 peppercorns (white or black)
1 teaspoon white wine vinegar	½ cup butter, cut into pieces
salt	

Fish

8-12 fresh red snapper fillets	oil
	julienned leeks
seafood seasoning for blackened seafood	julienned carrots

To prepare sauce: Combine shallots, wine, vinegar, salt, lemon juice and peppercorns in a heavy, enameled pan. Cook until liquid has almost evaporated, watching closely so mixture does not burn. Add butter to pan. Remove from heat and beat until sauce begins to thicken.

To prepare fish: Heat a cast iron skillet as hot as possible. Heavily season fillets and dip in oil, covering both sides. Cook quickly, turning once in hot skillet, (about 1-1½ minutes to brown each side). Transfer to a warm platter. Cover with sauce and garnish with vegetables. Serve immediately. *Serves 4-6.*

Leeks are very sandy. To clean, cut off most of the green top and slice leek in half lengthwise. Wash leeks under cold running water, separating the layers. Pat dry and slice as directed in recipe.

GRILLED RED FISH

¼	cup butter, melted	2	tomatoes, finely chopped
1	onion, minced	1	whole large red fish
1	clove garlic, minced		salt and pepper
2	Tablespoons chopped fresh parsley		parsley
1	Tablespoon Worcestershire sauce		lemon slices
¼	cup slivered almonds		
	juice of 1 lemon		

In a small saucepan, sauté onion and garlic in butter. Add parsley, Worcestershire, almonds, lemon juice and tomato. Cook until heated. Clean fish, leaving head and tail on. Sprinkle with salt and pepper. Place in a heavy iron skillet. Pour butter sauce over fish. Grill fish in skillet over medium-hot coals 15 minutes per pound or until fish flakes easily. (May be baked at 375° for 12-15 minutes.) Baste often with sauce as it cooks. Remove from fire and garnish with parsley and lemon slices. Serve with remaining sauce. *Serves 4.*

POACHED CHILLED SALMON

3	pounds salmon fillets or 6 1-inch thick salmon steaks	3	Tablespoons unsalted butter, cut into ½-inch pieces
	salt	2	large lemons, cut into wedges, seeds removed
10	black peppercorns		
10	allspice berries		

Cut the fillets into pieces 3-inches long. Sprinkle lightly with salt and place on the rack of a fish poacher. Scatter with spices. Add enough water to barely cover the fish. Dot with butter and arrange lemon wedges over the fish. Cover. Bring to a boil, then shift the lid so it partially covers the poacher. Simmer until the fish is done, 10-12 minutes per inch of fish measured at its thickest point. Remove fillets from stock, reserving stock. Transfer fillets to a platter. Cool, cover and chill. Remove lemon and spices from the stock. Cool and chill. To serve, remove fat from stock and spoon over fillets. *Serves 6.*

TURTLE CREEK SOLE

4	fresh sole fillets (8 ounces each)	¾	cup sour cream
½	medium onion, finely chopped	½	teaspoon dill weed
4	Tablespoons butter, melted		salt and pepper
			grated rind of 1 lemon
		1	Tablespoon fresh lemon juice

Preheat oven to 350°. Pat fillets dry and arrange in a 9x13-inch glass baking dish. In a saucepan, sauté onion in butter until most of the liquid has evaporated. Remove from heat. Stir in remaining ingredients. Spread over fillets. Bake 12-15 minutes or until fish flakes easily with a fork, being careful not to overbake. *Serves 4.*

"A buffet dinner is one where the guests outnumber the chairs."

RED SNAPPER WITH BANANA BUTTER

Banana Butter

½	ripe banana		pinch cayenne pepper
¼	cup butter		pinch tarragon

Snapper

3	Tablespoons chopped pimiento	¼-½	cup butter, melted
3	Tablespoons chopped capers		salt and pepper
2	Tablespoons butter, melted		*Banana butter*
4	fresh red snapper fillets, ½ pound each	½	cup sliced almonds
3	Tablespoons flour	1	Tablespoon chopped parsley
		1	Tablespoon butter, melted

To prepare butter: In a food processor fitted with a metal blade, blend all ingredients until smooth. Transfer mixture to a sheet of aluminum foil and shape mixture into a log. Freeze. When ready to use, unwrap and slice.

To prepare fish: In a small skillet, sauté pimiento and capers in 2 Tablespoons butter and set aside. Preheat oven to 500°. Lightly flour fillets. In a large, heavy skillet sauté fillets in ¼ cup butter, adding more as needed. When browned, transfer fillets to a shallow buttered casserole dish. Sprinkle with salt and pepper. Place several banana butter slices over fish. Sprinkle with pimiento and capers. Bake 4 minutes. While baking, sauté nuts and parsley in remaining butter. Remove fish from oven. Sprinkle with nuts and parsley. Serve immediately. *Serves 4.*

When cooking fish, calculate 10 minutes per inch of thickness, regardless of cooking technique used.

GRILLED FISH WITH GOLDEN SAUCE

Golden Sauce

½	cup unsalted butter, melted		salt and white pepper
3	medium shallots, minced	½	teaspoon cayenne pepper
1	cup white wine	1	Tablespoon fresh chopped parsley
3	cups whipping cream	2	cups cooked crab meat
12	egg yolks, beaten		

Fish

8	fish fillets (flounder, trout, etc.)		lemon juice
			melted butter

To prepare sauce: In a large saucepan, sauté shallots in butter. Stir in wine and cream. Bring to a boil. Remove from heat. Add yolks, salt, pepper and cayenne. Mix thoroughly. Stir in parsley and crab.

To prepare fish: Brush tops of fillets with lemon juice and butter. Grill over hot coals or under oven broiler until fish flakes easily. Remove from heat. Pour sauce over fillets and serve immediately. *Serves 6-8.*

SENSATIONAL SOLE

2	pounds fresh sole fillets	¼	cup butter, melted
2	Tablespoons fresh lemon juice	3	Tablespoons mayonnaise
dash	Tabasco sauce	3	Tablespoons chopped red onions
½	cup grated Parmesan cheese	¼	teaspoon salt

Place fillets in a large broiling pan and baste with lemon juice. Broil 6-8 minutes. While fish is broiling, make the topping by mixing remaining ingredients in a medium bowl. Remove fish from broiler. Spread with topping. Return to broiler and continue broiling 3 more minutes or until browned. *Serves 4.*

CRISP FISH WITH HOT BEAN SAUCE

Seasoning

1½ cups water	1 teaspoon Szechuan chili sauce
2 Tablespoons soy sauce	
2 Tablespoons sherry	¼ cup sugar
1 Tablespoon sweet bean paste	1 Tablespoon vinegar pepper
2 Tablespoons hot bean paste	1½ teaspoons cornstarch
	1 teaspoon flour

Fish

1½ pounds fish fillets (trout or snapper)	1 Tablespoon ginger, finely chopped
2 Tablespoons sherry	1 Tablespoon garlic, finely chopped
½ cup cornstarch	
½ cup flour	¼ cup scallions, chopped
oil	
2 scallions, finely chopped	

To prepare seasoning: In a medium bowl, combine all ingredients. To prepare fish: Sprinkle fish with sherry and marinate 20 minutes. Mix flour and cornstarch and coat fish well. In a wok or large skillet, heat oil to medium-high. Fry fish until golden and crisp, about 2-3 minutes per side. Remove fish and drain. Arrange on a serving platter and keep warm. Drain all but 3 Tablespoons of oil from wok. Add the 2 scallions, ginger and garlic. Stirring constantly, add the seasoning mixture. Bring to a boil and pour over fish. Sprinkle with remaining scallions. *Serves 4.*

FISH FILLETS WITH BEURRE BLANC SAUCE

3 pounds skinned and boned fresh fish fillets (salmon, sea bass, etc.)	

Beurre Blanc Sauce

3-5 shallots, finely chopped	1½ cups butter, softened to room temperature
¾ cup distilled or white wine vinegar	salt and white pepper

To prepare sauce: Place shallots and vinegar in a small saucepan. Cook over moderate high heat until liquid is reduced to 1 Tablespoon. (May be prepared several hours prior to serving at this point. When ready to complete, reheat mixture until pan is hot but not burning to the touch and proceed with recipe.) Whisk in butter, 2 Tablespoons at a time, adding more as previous addition melts. If pan becomes too hot, remove from heat or sauce will separate. Season to taste. Sauce may be kept warm in a double boiler.

To prepare fish: Broil fish until easily flaked. Place on a warm platter and cover with sauce. *Serves 6.*

Beurre Blanc creates a different flavor when some Noilly Prat Vermouth is added to the white wine. A large spoonful of fine caviar provides a flavorful touch.

SHRIMP SICILY

1½ pounds fresh large shrimp, peeled and deveined
¼ cup flour
salt and pepper
3 Tablespoons butter, melted
3 Tablespoons olive oil
2 large cloves garlic, minced
2 teaspoons dried oregano
2 Tablespoons chopped parsley
juice of 1 lemon

Pat shrimp dry on paper towels. In a small bowl, season flour with salt and pepper. In a large skillet, heat butter and oil with garlic and oregano over medium-high heat. Lightly flour shrimp, then quickly stir-fry in hot oil, reducing heat as necessary. Shrimp should begin to become firm and turn pink in 4-5 minutes depending on their size. Immediately before removing shrimp from skillet, stir in parsley and lemon juice. Serve immediately. *Serves 4.*

FIERY CAJUN SHRIMP

1 cup butter, melted
1 cup margarine, melted
⅜-½ cup Worcestershire sauce
4 Tablespoons pepper
1 teaspoon ground rosemary
2 teaspoons Tabasco
2 teaspoons sea salt
3 cloves garlic, minced
juice of 2 lemons
2 lemons, thinly sliced
5-6 pounds unpeeled shrimp

Preheat oven to 400°. In a medium bowl, mix all ingredients except shrimp and lemon slices. Pour ½ cup butter mixture to cover the bottom of a large baking dish. Arrange layers of shrimp and lemon slices over butter, up to one inch from top of dish. Pour remaining butter over layers. Bake, uncovered, stirring once or twice for 10 minutes. Continue baking 5-10 minutes if needed. *Serves 8-10.*

SCALLOPS AND SHRIMP

¼ cup butter, melted
1 clove garlic, minced
½ cup sliced scallions
1 pound medium shrimp, peeled
1 pound fresh scallops
1 pound mushrooms
juice of 1 lemon
½ teaspoon dill weed
⅛ teaspoon cayenne pepper
1½ ounces dry vermouth

In a large skillet, sauté garlic, scallions, shrimp and scallops in butter for 3 minutes. Add mushrooms and continue to sauté 2 minutes. Stir in remaining ingredients and simmer 5 minutes. Serve immediately. *Serves 4.*

SHRIMP KIEV

½ cup butter, softened
1 Tablespoon basil, finely chopped
1 Tablespoon parsley, finely chopped
2 cloves garlic, finely minced

12 jumbo shrimp
flour
1 egg, beaten
dry bread crumbs
oil

In a food processor fitted with the metal blade, blend butter, herbs and garlic. Transfer to a small bowl and chill several hours. At least 3 hours before serving, peel and devein shrimp, leaving the tails on 6 of the shrimp. Butterfly all the shrimp, being careful not to cut all the way through. With the flat side of a large knife, flatten all shrimp. Place a teaspoon of the butter in the center of the 6 shrimp with the tails on. Top with remaining shrimp, pressing edges to seal. Dredge shrimp in flour and dip in egg. Coat completely with crumbs, pressing with fingers to form a complete seal around the butter. Place shrimp on waxed paper and freeze at least one hour. To cook, thaw slightly until just firm to the touch. In a deep fryer or pan with enough oil to cover shrimp, heat oil until hot but not smoking. Cook shrimp 2½-3 minutes or until golden brown. Serve immediately. *Makes 6 kievs; Serves 2-3.*

Freeze fresh leaf herbs such as chervil or tarragon for winter substitutes for dried.

SHRIMP VALENCIA

½ cup butter, melted
½ cup minced green onions
20 mushroom caps
3 14-ounce cans artichoke hearts, drained
1½ -2 cups chicken broth

juice of 2 lemons
4 Tablespoons flour
salt and white pepper
24 cherry tomatoes
2 pounds shrimp, cooked and peeled
1 cup pitted black olives

In a large saucepan, sauté onion in butter. Add mushrooms and continue to sauté. Stir in artichoke hearts, lemon juice and 1 cup broth. Simmer. In a small bowl, combine ½ cup broth, flour, salt and pepper to taste and add to mushroom mixture. Simmer until sauce thickens slightly. If sauce becomes too thick, stir in more broth. Fold in tomatoes, shrimp and olives, being careful not to crush tomatoes. Heat thoroughly. *Serves 8-10.*

SEAFOOD SOUFFLÉ

grated Parmesan cheese
1 pound fresh peeled shrimp or crab meat
4 eggs
4 ounces sharp cheese, cubed
3 ounces cream cheese

¼ cup milk
¼ cup grated Parmesan cheese
1 teaspoon minced onion
½ teaspoon dill
½ teaspoon lemon juice

Preheat oven to 350°. Butter a 4-cup soufflé dish and sprinkle with Parmesan. Set aside. In a food processor fitted with the metal blade or in a blender, combine remaining ingredients and process until well-blended. Pour into a prepared dish and bake 40-45 minutes. The center will be runny and can be used as a sauce for the remaining soufflé. *Serves 4.*

VEGETABLES

CHIMAYO CORN PUDDING

1½	cups creamed corn	2	eggs, beaten
1	cup yellow corn meal	½	teaspoon baking soda
1	cup butter, melted	2	cups grated Cheddar
¾	cup milk		cheese
2	medium onions,	1	4-ounce can chopped
	chopped		green chilies

Preheat oven to 350°. In a large bowl, combine corn, corn meal, butter, milk, onions, eggs and soda. Pour ½ of the batter into a greased 9-inch square baking pan. Cover evenly with ½ of the cheese, all the chilies and then the remaining cheese. Top with remaining batter. Bake 1 hour. Let cool 10 minutes before serving. Serves 8.

GRILLED CORN WITH CHILI BUTTER

1	teaspoon chili powder
½	cup salted butter
4	ears fresh corn

To prepare butter: In a food processor fitted with metal blade, process chili powder and butter until smooth.

To prepare corn: Pull husks down from corn but do not remove. Discard silk. Spread each ear with 1 Tablespoon chili butter. Pull husks up and wrap in foil. Grill over hot coals for 40 minutes, turning often. Serve hot with remaining butter. Serves 4.

There is a separate silk strand for each kernel on an ear of corn.

SAUTÉED BABY VEGETABLES

16	baby carrots	16	baby patty-pan squash
16	baby zucchini or	8	Tablespoons butter
	yellow squash		salt and pepper
16	baby turnips		

Leaving ½-inch stem on, peel carrots and turnips. Blanch each vegetable separately in boiling salted water until tender crisp. Plunge into cold water, drain and dry on paper towels. Shortly before serving, melt butter in large skillet and gently sauté vegetables until warmed thoroughly. Season to taste with salt and pepper and serve immediately. Serves 8.

Sprinkle gratings of the peel of any citrus fruit over vegetables, salads and fruits for a low calorie seasoning.

BROCCOLI WITH BLEU CHEESE

1	pound broccoli
	buttered fresh bread crumbs

Sauce

2	Tablespoons butter,	1	cup milk
	melted	3	ounces cream cheese
2	Tablespoons flour	2	ounces bleu cheese

Preheat oven to 325°. Steam broccoli until tender crisp. Drain and cut into 2-inch pieces. Place pieces in a greased baking dish. Cover with hot sauce and sprinkle with crumbs. Bake 20 minutes. Serves 6.

To prepare sauce: In a medium skillet, whisk flour with butter and cook 1 minute over medium heat. Slowly whisk in milk. Cook until thick and smooth, 4-5 minutes. Add cheeses and stir until melted.

RED PEPPER TIMBALES

2¼ cups red bell pepper, peeled, seeded and finely diced
⅛ cup onion, finely diced
1 teaspoon butter, melted
8 extra large eggs, slightly beaten
4 dashes Tabasco
1 teaspoon sugar
1 teaspoon herbs de provence
1 teaspoon fresh lemon juice
pinch of dried mint
pinch of nutmeg
1 teaspoon salt
pepper
1½ cups whipping cream

To peel peppers: Grill or broil until peppers are blackened on all sides. Place in a paper bag and allow to steam in the bag 5 minutes. Remove from bag and peel off skins.

Preheat oven to 325°. In a small skillet, sauté onion in butter 1-2 minutes. Transfer to a large bowl and add peppers, eggs and seasonings. Mix well. In a separate bowl, lightly whip cream to consistency of thick buttermilk. Fold cream into pepper mixture. Spoon into buttered timbale mold to just below the rims. Place molds on a thin towel in a bain marie (water bath). Bring water to a boil on top of the stove. Transfer to oven and bake 25 minutes. Remove molds from water bath and let rest 10 minutes before removing from mold. *Serves 12.*

GREEN CHILI SPOONBREAD

½ cup yellow cornmeal
1½ cups boiling water
2 Tablespoons butter, softened
8 large eggs, beaten for 3 minutes
1 cup whipping cream
½ teaspoon salt
½ cup diced green chilies, drained
1 Tablespoon baking powder
¼ cup grated Parmesan cheese
picante sauce or salsa

In a large bowl, place cornmeal and cover with boiling water. Stir well to remove lumps. Let stand 5 minutes. Butter an 8x11-inch baking dish. Add butter, eggs cream, salt, chilies, baking powder and cheese to cornmeal. Pour into prepared dish. Let stand 30 minutes. To serve, preheat oven to 350°. Bake 45 minutes or until puffed and golden brown. Cut into squares and serve with sauce. *Serves 6-8.*

EGGS TIMBALE

5 eggs, beaten well
1½ cups milk
1 teaspoon parsley, finely chopped
1 teaspoon onion juice
1 teaspoon salt
¼ teaspoon paprika

Preheat oven to 325°. In a large bowl, mix all ingredients until well blended. Pour into 5 greased custard cups. Place cups in a pan of hot water. Bake 45 minutes. *Serves 5.*

Note: As a variation, top with cooked lobster, shrimp or fresh mushroom sauce flavored with sherry.

Eggs will separate better if chilled, but for largest volume, egg whites should be at room temperature when beaten.

FRUIT, NUT AND SAUSAGE STUFFING

1	cup golden raisins	2	Tablespoons olive oil
1	cup chopped dried apricot halves	1	pound bulk pork sausage
1	cup dark raisins	3	cups seasoned bread crumbs or seasoned cornmeal
1	cup bourbon		
2½	cups chopped celery stalk and leaves	2	teaspoons pepper
2	yellow onions, chopped	2	teaspoons thyme
		3	eggs, beaten
3	tart green apples, unpeeled, cored and chopped	2½	cups chicken broth
		½	cup butter, melted (optional)
¼-½	cup butter, melted	1	20-25 pound turkey
2	cups coarsely chopped unsalted nuts (pecans)		

Preheat oven to 325°. In a small saucepan, combine all raisins, apricots and bourbon. Bring to a boil. Remove from heat. Cover and set aside. In a large skillet, gently sauté celery, onions and apples in ¼-½ cup butter over medium-high heat for 10 minutes or until tender. Transfer to a large bowl. In the same skillet, sauté nuts in oil until golden. Add to onion mixture. In the skillet, brown sausage, stirring over medium-high heat until meat has crumbled and no pink remains. Add to onion mixture. Drain raisins and apricots. Add to onions. Stir in crumbs or cornmeal, pepper and thyme. Mix thoroughly. Gently mix in ⅓ of the beaten eggs and 1 cup of the broth. Add remaining egg and broth. Mix gently. (Optional: Stir in remaining butter.) Loosely stuff turkey with stuffing. Bake 6-7 hours or according to turkey package instructions. Place remainder of stuffing in a greased baking dish and bake 30 minutes before serving. *Serves 12.*

GREEN BEANS SUPREME

1	large onion, thinly sliced	1	cup sour cream
		1	cup plain yogurt
½	cup snipped fresh parsley	10	cups fresh French-cut green beans, cooked
1	Tablespoon butter, melted	1	cup grated cheese (American, Swiss or Cheddar)
¾	Tablespoons whole wheat flour		
salt		¾	Tablespoons butter, melted
Worcestershire sauce		1	cup seasoned bread crumbs
garlic pepper			
2	teaspoons grated lemon peel		

In a large skillet, sauté onions and parsley in butter until soft. Stir in flour, seasonings, peel, sour cream and yogurt. Add green beans and mix well. Spoon into a greased 2-quart casserole dish. Sprinkle with cheese. Stir crumbs into remaining butter. Sprinkle on top of cheese. Bake 20-25 minutes or until heated through. *Serves 10-12.*

JALAPEÑO CORN

4	3-ounce packages cream cheese	3-4	fresh jalapeños, seeded and chopped
½	cup milk	4	12-ounce cans white shoepeg corn, drained
4	Tablespoons butter		
1	teaspoon garlic salt	butter	

Preheat oven to 350°. In a medium saucepan, place cheese, milk, butter and salt. Cook over low heat, stirring until cheese and butter melt, forming a sauce. Remove from heat. Mix in jalapeños and corn. Pour into a 9x12-inch glass baking dish. Dot with butter. Bake 30 minutes or until bubbly. *Serves 6-8.*

ASPARAGUS VINAIGRETTE

Vinaigrette Sauce

1	teaspoon salt	dash Worcestershire sauce	
½	teaspoon pepper	dash Tabasco	
½	teaspoon garlic, finely minced	3	Tablespoons tarragon vinegar
¼	teaspoon sugar	10	Tablespoons salad oil
½	teaspoon dry mustard	2	Tablespoons whipping cream
1	teaspoon Dijon mustard		
⅛	teaspoon cayenne pepper	2	teaspoons parsley, chopped
24	fresh asparagus spears, trimmed		

To prepare sauce: Combine all ingredients in a jar. Shake well and chill. To serve: Steam asparagus until tender but still crisp. Drain and arrange on individual plates. Drizzle cold sauce over tips. *Serves 4.*

JULIENNED ZUCCHINI IN GARLIC BUTTER

1	pound zucchini, julienned	2	Tablespoons fresh parsley, chopped
2	Tablespoons olive oil	½	teaspoon dried thyme
1	clove garlic, finely chopped		freshly ground black pepper
1	shallot, finely chopped		

Heat oil over low heat and sauté garlic and shallot for 1 minute. Add remaining ingredients and cook 5-8 minutes until zucchini is crisp-tender. *Serves 4.*

HERBED ZUCCHINI WITH SWISS CHEESE

4	cups thinly sliced zucchini	¼	teaspoon garlic powder
1	cup chopped onions	¼	teaspoon basil
¼-½	cup butter, melted	¼	teaspoon oregano
½	cup chopped parsley	2	eggs, beaten
½	teaspoon salt	2	cups grated Swiss cheese
½	teaspoon pepper		

Preheat oven to 375°. In a large skillet, sauté zucchini and onions in ¼ cup butter, adding more butter as necessary. Transfer mixture to a large bowl. Blend in remaining ingredients. Spoon into a greased 1½-quart rectangular casserole dish. Bake 20-25 minutes. Remove from oven and let stand 15 minutes before serving. *Serves 6.*

SPINACH INTRIGUE

2	10-ounce packages frozen chopped spinach	½	cup butter, melted
4	Tablespoons finely chopped onions	2	6-ounce cans tomato paste
¼	pound fresh mushrooms, sliced	2	cups sour cream
			paprika

Preheat oven to 350°. Cook spinach according to package instructions and drain thoroughly. In a small skillet, sauté onions and mushrooms in butter. Place spinach in a 1½-quart casserole dish. Lightly, but thoroughly, mix in mushroom mixture. Spread tomato paste over spinach, then cover with a thin layer of sour cream. Sprinkle with paprika. Bake 20-30 minutes until heated thoroughly. *Serves 8.*

"A meal without cheese is like a beautiful woman with only one eye."

BAKED PURÉED CARROTS

1	pound carrots	½	teaspoon salt
2	Tablespoons finely chopped onions	1	Tablespoon flour
½	green bell pepper, diced (optional)	1	Tablespoon sugar
		1	cup milk
2	Tablespoons butter, melted		

Preheat oven to 350°. In a medium saucepan, cover carrots with water. Add a pinch of salt and bring to a boil. Cook 20 minutes or until tender. Sauté onions and bell pepper (if desired) in butter until onion is golden. Blend in salt, flour and sugar. Mix in milk. In a food processor fitted with a metal blade, purée the cooked carrots. Add onion mixture. Pour into greased 1-quart casserole dish and bake 30 minutes. *Serves 6.*

BROILED EGGPLANT WITH GARLIC

3	cloves garlic, finely chopped		salt and pepper
½	cup olive oil	1	cup freshly grated Parmesan cheese
1	large or 2 small, unpeeled eggplants	¼	cup parsley, finely chopped

In a small bowl, combine garlic and oil. Let stand 1 hour. Slice eggplant into ½-inch thick rounds. When ready to serve, place oven rack on the middle shelf and preheat broiler. Place eggplant on a greased baking sheet. Brush with the oil and season with salt and pepper. Broil 5 minutes. Turn slices over and brush with oil and broil 3-4 more minutes. Top with cheese and continue to broil 2 minutes or until browned. Sprinkle with parsley and serve. *Serves 4.*

MINTED CARROTS

1	pound carrots, sliced in ¼-inch rounds	2	Tablespoons honey
3	Tablespoons butter	1-2	Tablespoons fresh chopped mint

Cook carrots in boiling salted water until tender, about 20 minutes. Drain and return to saucepan. Over low heat, add butter and honey to carrots and toss until well coated. Remove from heat, toss mint with carrots and serve immediately. *Serves 4.*

SAUSAGE BLACK-EYED PEAS

1	pound hot sausage	1	clove garlic, pressed
4	cups cooked black-eyed peas	1	16-ounce can tomatoes
1	medium onion, chopped	¼	cup water
		1	teaspoon chili powder
½-1	green bell pepper, chopped	¼	teaspoon pepper

In a large saucepan, brown sausage, stirring over medium-high heat until meat has crumbled and no pink remains. Pour off fat. Mix in remaining ingredients and simmer 1 hour. *Serves 10-12.*

SAUTÉED SPINACH WITH PINE NUTS

4	Tablespoons butter	2	pounds fresh spinach, rinsed and trimmed
1	large clove garlic, finely minced	½	cup toasted pine nuts

In a large skillet, melt butter over medium heat. Add garlic and sauté briefly. Add spinach to fill skillet and sauté until wilted. Continue adding spinach in batches until all is wilted. Toss in pine nuts and serve immediately. *Serves 4.*

POTATOES CHANTILLY

4 potatoes, peeled and sliced	2 cups whipping cream
8 ounces grated Swiss cheese	2 cloves garlic
2 cups half-and-half cream	salt and pepper

Preheat oven to 350°. Soak potatoes briefly in cold water. In a large saucepan, heat both creams with garlic. Do not boil. Remove garlic and discard. Drain potatoes and pat dry with paper towels. In a 3-quart soufflé or deep casserole dish, layer potatoes and cheese until all are used. Pour cream mixture to top of potatoes. Cover and bake 2 hours. Uncover and bake 1 additional hour. *Serves 8.*

Soaking sliced or diced potatoes in cold water keeps them from turning gray and draws out some of the starch preventing glue-like dishes. Be sure to pat dry on paper towels before proceeding with the recipe.

OVEN ROASTED POTATOES

3-4 medium potatoes, unpeeled	½ teaspoon paprika
¼ cup butter, melted	garlic salt
	pepper

Preheat oven to 450°. Slice potatoes in the shape of large French fries. Soak in cold, salted water for 15 minutes. Dry on paper towels. In a large bowl, toss potatoes with butter to coat well. Spread potatoes with butter in a 9x13-inch shallow baking pan. Sprinkle with paprika and seasonings. Bake 30-40 minutes, turning several times until browned. Drain on paper towels and serve immediately. *Serves 4.*

THE WORKS POTATO BAKE

4 large red-skinned boiling potatoes, unpeeled	¼ cup milk
8 slices bacon	1 bunch green onions, chopped
1 teaspoon salt	2 cups sour cream
½ teaspoon pepper	1 heaping cup grated American cheese
4 Tablespoons butter	

Preheat oven to 300°. In a large pot, boil potatoes in water to cover until tender, about 45 minutes. While cooking, fry bacon until crisp in a large skillet. Drain well. Crumble and set aside. When potatoes are finished, drain and add salt, pepper, butter and milk. Mash. Add half of onions and bacon. Stir in ½ cup sour cream and mix well. Spoon mixture into a 9½x11-inch glass baking dish. Cover with remaining sour cream, cheese and bacon. Cover dish and bake 15-20 minutes or until cheese melts. Garnish with remaining onions. *Serves 6.*

POTATOES SUPREME

6 medium red potatoes	10 ounces sharp Cheddar cheese, grated
1½ cups whipping cream	
salt and pepper	

Cook potatoes in boiling salted water until tender, about 25 minutes. Refrigerate in their jackets overnight. Preheat oven to 350°. Peel potatoes and grate in food processor. Grease a 2-quart deep casserole. Whip cream until it has body, but is not stiff. Place a layer of potatoes in casserole and season to taste with salt and pepper. Cover potatoes with one third of cream followed by one third of cheese. Repeat layers two more times. Bake for 30 minutes until bubbly. *Serves 8.*

Pasta And Rice

FETTUCINI IN WINE CREAM SAUCE WITH SAUSAGE

1	pound sweet Italian sausage	¼	cup freshly grated Parmesan cheese
2	Tablespoons butter	¼	teaspoon nutmeg
1	Tablespoon olive oil		salt
1	cup chopped onions		white pepper
1	cup dry white wine	¼	cup butter
1	teaspoon thyme	1	pound fettucini
2	whole cloves		grated Parmesan cheese
1	cup whipping cream		cayenne pepper

Remove sausage from casings. Crumble and sauté in a large skillet over moderate heat. Cook until well done. Drain and discard fat. Return to skillet along with butter and oil. Add onions and sauté. Stir in wine, thyme and cloves. Cover and simmer over low heat for 30 minutes. Discard cloves. Mix in cream, cheese, nutmeg and seasonings. Cook over moderate heat until cream thickens, 3-5 minutes. To serve, place hot pasta cooked al dente and drained and remaining butter in a 2½-quart bowl. Toss well and spoon onto warmed plates. Top with sausage mixture. Sprinkle with Parmesan and cayenne. *Serves 6.*

RED PASTA WITH GOAT CHEESE AND CREAM SAUCE

Cream Sauce

2½	cups whipping cream	5	sprigs fresh parsley, minced
12	cloves garlic, lightly crushed		fresh red peppers or cherry tomatoes
5	ounces goat cheese		
	white pepper		
1	pound fresh red pasta		

To prepare sauce: In a saucepan, bring cream to a boil. Add garlic. Reduce heat and simmer 20 minutes. Remove garlic and discard. In a food processor fitted with a metal blade, purée half of the cream with the cheese. With machine running, process in remaining cream and pepper to taste.

To serve: Toss hot pasta cooked al dente and drained with sauce and parsley. Garnish with peppers or tomatoes. *Serves 4.*

PASTA TRICOLORE

½	cup extra virgin olive oil	2	Tablespoons parsley, chopped
2	cloves garlic, minced	8	ounces goat cheese, crumbled
½	onion, cut into thin rings	½	cup grated Parmesan cheese
3	red bell peppers, cut into julienne strips		salt and pepper
1	pound fresh spinach pasta (tube or shell-shape)		

In a medium skillet, sauté garlic, onion and pepper strips in oil over low heat until soft. Place hot pasta cooked al dente and drained on a large serving platter. Cover with pepper mixture and toss well. Add remaining ingredients and toss again. Serve immediately. *Serves 4.*

PRIMA PASTA

½ cup unsalted butter
1 clove garlic, crushed
1 head cauliflower, cut into flowerettes
1 bunch broccoli, cut into flowerettes
3 medium zucchini, sliced ¼-inch thick
3 large, firm tomatoes, unpeeled, seeded and chopped
1½ cups fresh snow peas, blanched
1 teaspoon salt
black pepper
1½ cups half-and-half cream
1 12-ounce package large macaroni (seashell)
½ cup grated Romano cheese
½ cup grated Parmesan cheese

In a very large skillet, melt butter and add garlic. When butter begins to foam, discard garlic. Mix in vegetables except snow peas. Stir-fry 1 minute. Cover and cook over medium heat 3 minutes. Blend in salt, pepper and cream. Bring to a boil. Mix in snow peas and pasta cooked al dente and drained. Blend well. Toss with cheeses and serve immediately. *Serves 12.*

HAY AND STRAW FETTUCINI WITH RED PEPPER AND MUSHROOM SAUCE

Sauce

½ cup butter, melted
3 cloves garlic, minced
2 red bell peppers, cut into 1x¼-inch strips
1 pound fresh mushrooms, sliced
½ pound fresh spinach pasta
½ cup beef broth
¾ cup whipping cream
salt
freshly grated Parmesan cheese
½ pound fresh plain pasta

To prepare sauce: In a large, heavy skillet sauté garlic in butter. Stir in peppers and sauté until they are beginning to soften. Stir in mushrooms and cook until soft. Blend in broth and simmer 20 minutes. (May be prepared ahead and chilled up to 24 hours at this point.) Add cream and simmer until slightly thickened, about 5 minutes. Season with salt.

To serve: In a large bowl toss hot pasta cooked al dente and drained with sauce. Divide among plates and top with Parmesan. *Serves 8 as a first course; 4-6 as an entrée.*

PASTA CARBONARA

4 eggs
¾ cup half-and-half cream
½ cup chopped fresh parsley
½ cup freshly grated Parmesan cheese
½ cup freshly grated Romano cheese
1 pound fresh mushrooms, sliced
2 Tablespoons olive oil
½ pound bacon, cut in large pieces
1-2 large onions
1 pound fresh linguine
cayenne pepper
Parmesan cheese

In a small bowl, blend eggs, cream, parsley and cheeses and bring to room temperature. In a medium skillet, sauté mushrooms in oil. In a large skillet, cook bacon until soft. Remove bacon, reserving rendered fat. Set aside. In reserved fat, sauté onions. Combine onions, bacon and mushrooms. Spoon over hot pasta cooked al dente and drained, followed by cream mixture. Toss well. Sprinkle with pepper and serve accompanied with additional Parmesan. *Serves 6-8.*

NUTTED WILD RICE

1	cup wild rice	5	Tablespoons butter
2	cups chicken stock, boiling	4	shallots, minced
2	Tablespoons unsalted butter	¼	pound mushrooms, quartered
1	cup brown rice		salt and pepper
2⅔	cups chicken stock, boiling	1	cup pecan halves
		½	cup chopped fresh parsley

In the top of a double boiler over simmering water, cook the wild rice in 2 cups boiling stock and 2 Tablespoons butter for one hour, covered. Place brown rice, 2⅔ cups boiling stock and 2 Tablespoons butter in medium saucepan and bring to a boil. Reduce heat to low and cook until all water is absorbed, about 50 minutes. Melt remaining 3 Tablespoons butter in a medium skillet over medium heat and sauté shallots and mushrooms for 5 minutes. Toss wild rice, brown rice and mushrooms together in a large bowl. Season to taste with salt and pepper. (Can be prepared in advance to this point; reheat in the top of a double boiler over simmering water.) Add pecans and parsley and mix thoroughly. *Serves 8 to 10.*

FRIED RICE WITH SPINACH

3	Tablespoons peanut oil	3	eggs, beaten
⅓	pound mushrooms, thinly sliced	3	cups cooked rice
4	green onions (green parts) cut into 1-inch slices	3	Tablespoons soy sauce
		¼	cup chopped cilantro
1	cup shredded carrots		
1	pound fresh spinach, coarsely chopped, or 1 10 ounce package frozen chopped spinach, thawed and well-drained		

In a large skillet, heat oil over medium-high heat. Add mushrooms, onions and carrots. Cook, stirring often, until tender, 3 to 5 minutes. Add spinach. Cover and cook 1 minute. Reduce heat to medium and uncover. Add eggs, stirring constantly for 2 minutes until eggs are cooked and spinach is wilted. Add rice, soy sauce and cilantro. Stir until mixture is heated thoroughly. *Serves 8.*

MIDDLE EASTERN BROWN RICE

1½	cups brown rice	1	cup pine nuts
3¾	cups water or chicken broth	1	teaspoon paprika
		¼	teaspoon Tabasco sauce
1¼	Tablespoon butter	¾-1	teaspoon salt
1¼	teaspoons salt	½	teaspoon pepper
½	cup olive oil	¼	cup fresh parsley, chopped
1	cup onions, finely chopped		
		3-4	pimientos, chopped

In a large saucepan, combine rice, broth, butter and 1¼ teaspoons salt. Bring to a boil, stirring a few times. Cover and reduce heat. Simmer 30-45 minutes. (For a drier rice, remove from heat after cooking, fluff with a fork, and let stand covered 5-10 minutes.) While rice is cooking, heat oil in a large saucepan and lightly sauté onions, nuts, paprika and Tabasco. To serve, toss rice with onions. Season with remaining salt and pepper. Garnish with parsley and pimientos. *Serves 6.*

BAKED RICE AND SAUSAGE

½	pound pork sausage	½-¾	cup soy sauce
3	cups cooked white rice, chilled	¾	cup green onion tops, chopped

Preheat oven to 350°. In a large skillet, brown sausage, breaking up large pieces as it cooks. Drain fat, reserving 3 Tablespoons. Carefully mix in rice. Cook over low heat until hot. Blend in soy sauce to coat rice. Spoon into a large casserole dish. Cover and bake 30 minutes. Remove from oven and fold in onions. *Serves 6.*

RAINBOW RICE

1	cup chopped onion	½	teaspoon dried whole saffron, crushed or ¼ teaspoon ground saffron
1	green pepper, chopped		
½	red pepper, chopped		
½	yellow pepper, chopped		
¼	cup peanut oil	2	small zucchini, cut into 1-inch pieces
1½	cups uncooked rice		
3½	cups chicken broth	¾	pound broccoli, cut into 1-inch pieces
2	ripe tomatoes, peeled and chopped		
		12	fresh or frozen asparagus spears, cut in 1-inch pieces
1	Tablespoon tomato paste		
¼	teaspoon salt	1	10-ounce package frozen English peas, defrosted
½	teaspoon pepper		
dash Worchestershire sauce			

Preheat oven to 350°. In Dutch oven, sauté onion and peppers in oil until tender. Stir in rice, broth, tomatoes, tomato paste, salt, pepper, Worcestershire and saffron. Bring to a boil. Remove from heat. Cover and bake 20 minutes. Remove from oven and stir in zucchini, broccoli and asparagus. Cover. Bake 30 more minutes or until liquid is absorbed and vegetables are tender but still crisp. Add peas, toss and serve. *Serves 10-12.*

When choosing fresh mushrooms, look for firm, pale mushrooms whose caps are closed — gills underneath should not show. Store in brown paper bags as plastic traps moisture.

TEXAS PASTA SALAD

1	pound pasta (Texas or wagon wheel-shaped or fusilli), cooked and drained
⅔	cup cider vinegar
¼	cup safflower oil
¾	cup chopped celery
¾	cup chopped green pepper
8	green onions, chopped
1	2-ounce jar chopped pimientos, drained
4	dashes Worcestershire sauce
4	dashes Tabasco
2	Tablespoons chopped green chilies
1	teaspoon salt
1½	teaspoons pepper
2	cups black-eyed peas, cooked and drained
1½	cups corn, cooked and drained
6	ounces ripe olives, chopped and drained
2	ounces green olives, chopped and drained
1	cup mayonnaise
2	Tablespoons picante sauce

In a large bowl, mix all ingredients. Chill at least 24 hours.
Serves 12.

FETTUCINE WITH CAVIAR

2	cups sour cream
½	cup whipping cream
¾	cup unsalted butter
6	Tablespoons lemon juice
1	pound fettucine
8	Tablespoons caviar
1	cup grated Parmesan cheese

In a medium saucepan, cook sour cream, cream and butter over low heat until it simmers and the butter melts. Add lemon juice. Cook fettucine in boiling salted water to al dente stage and drain. Gently fold caviar into sauce. Pour over hot pasta. Toss with cheese.
Serves 8.

PASTA SALAD WITH SMOKED TURKEY, FRESH ASPARAGUS AND RED PEPPER

Dressing

2	cloves garlic, crushed
2	small shallots, minced
2	large eggs
1	cup extra virgin olive oil
3	Tablespoons balsamic vinegar
½	teaspoon herbs de Provence
	salt and pepper

Salad

1	pound fresh asparagus, steamed, tender-crisp
1	red bell pepper, cut into 1-inch strips and steamed, tender-crisp
1½	cups smoked turkey, cut into pieces
1	pound Rotelle pasta or egg noodles
½	cup grated Parmesan cheese

To prepare dressing: Drop garlic into food processor fitted with the metal blade with machine running. Process in shallots, eggs and 2 Tablespoons oil. Blend well. Add vinegar, herbs and seasonings. With motor still running, slowly add remaining oil. Transfer to a bowl and let stand several hours.

To prepare salad: In a large bowl, cut asparagus diagonally into 1-inch pieces. Toss with pepper, turkey, pasta cooked al dente and drained, cheese and dressing. Serve immediately. *Serves 8.*

When choosing asparagus, the tips should be tightly closed and the stalks firm and green.

SPINACH PASTA WITH SMOKED SALMON SAUCE

6	Tablespoons butter, melted	4	ounces smoked salmon, shredded
2	Tablespoons finely chopped shallots	1	pound fresh spinach fettucini
1/4	cup tomato sauce		grated Parmesan cheese
2	cups whipping cream		

In a saucepan, sauté shallots in butter. Stir in tomato sauce and cook briefly. Add cream and simmer until thickened. Stir in salmon and heat thoroughly. Transfer sauce to a large bowl and toss with hot pasta, cooked al dente and drained. Serve immediately with cheese as an accompaniment. *Serves 4 as a main dish, 6-8 as an appetizer.*

FETTUCINI WITH RED CLAM SAUCE

4	ounces tomato paste	1	Tablespoon dried summer savory
1	8-ounce bottle clam juice	4	cloves garlic, minced
1/4	cup olive oil	3	cups sliced mushrooms
1	small onion, chopped	2	cups tomato sauce
1/2	cup chopped fresh parsley	1	pound fresh clams, chopped and drained
1	Tablespoon dried basil	1	pound fettucini noodles,
1	Tablespoon dried oregano		grated Parmesan cheese

In a small bowl, whisk tomato paste with clam juice and set aside. In a medium skillet, sauté onion, parsley, spices, garlic and mushrooms in oil until onions are soft. Stir in tomato sauce and clam juice mixture. Simmer 5 minutes. To serve, add fresh clams. Pour over hot pasta cooked al dente and drained. Sprinkle with cheese. *Serves 4.*

PASTA WITH TOMATO CREAM SAUCE

Tomato Sauce

1/2	pound smoked bacon, thickly sliced	2	large cloves garlic, minced
1	28-ounce can Italian tomatoes with basil, coarsely chopped	1	teaspoon dried and crumbled leaf sage

Cream Sauce

1/2	cup butter, melted	1	cup freshly grated Parmesan cheese
1 1/4	cups whipping cream		
1	pound penne pasta		

To prepare tomato sauce: Dice bacon into small pieces. In a large skillet, sauté bacon. Pour off fat. Stir in remaining ingredients. Cook over medium heat, uncovered, 20 minutes or until sauce is slightly thickened.

To prepare cream sauce: In a small saucepan, combine cream with butter over medium heat. Stir in cheese until melted.

To serve: In a large bowl, toss hot pasta cooked al dente and drained with cream sauce and then with tomato sauce. Serve immediately. *Serves 4-6 as an entree, 10-12 as a first course.*

DESSERTS

CHOCOLATE PARADISE PIE

Crust

3	egg whites	10	soda crackers,
1	cup sugar		crumbled
½	cup pecan halves	¼	teaspoon salt

Filling

1	cup semi-sweet chocolate chips		pinch of salt
3	egg yolks	¾	cup milk
1	Tablespoon Kahlua or	1	cup whipping cream, whipped
	½ teaspoon vanilla extract		semi-sweet chocolate shavings

To prepare crust: Preheat oven to 300°. In a large bowl (not plastic), beat whites until stiff but not dry. Gradually beat in sugar and salt until smooth. Fold in crackers and nuts. Spoon into the bottom of a greased 9-inch glass baking dish. Form into the shape of the pan but do not cover the edges. Bake 35-40 minutes.

To prepare filling: In a blender, place chocolate, yolks, liqueur and salt. Heat milk just to boiling point and add to blender. Blend on low 1 minute. Pour into prepared crust and chill until firm. To serve, spread whipped cream on top of pie. Sprinkle with shavings and cut into wedges. *Serves 8-10.*

Crème fraîche is cultured heavy cream. It thickens as it develops and has a slightly sour taste. It is more versatile than whipping cream because it does not separate when boiled. Use it with fresh fruit, in salad dressings, and in sauce making. It will keep in the refrigerator for two weeks.

WHITE CHOCOLATE LAYER CAKE

Cake

¼	pound white chocolate	2½	cups flour
½	cup boiling water	1	teaspoon baking powder
1	cup butter	1	cup buttermilk
2	cups sugar	1	cup chopped pecans
4	eggs, separated	1	cup flaked coconut
1	teaspoon vanilla		

Icing

½	cup butter	1½	teaspoons vanilla
2	3-ounce packages cream cheese, softened	½	cup chopped pecans
1	pound powdered sugar		milk

To prepare cake: Preheat oven to 350°. In a small saucepan over low heat, melt chocolate in water. In a large bowl, cream butter with sugar. Beat in yolks one at a time. Add chocolate mixture and vanilla. Sift together flour and baking powder. Add dry ingredients to chocolate mixture alternately with buttermilk. Do not overbeat. In a separate bowl, beat egg whites until stiff but not dry; fold into chocolate. Gently stir in remaining ingredients. Pour into 3 9-inch round, greased and floured cake pans. Bake 35-40 minutes. Cool slightly. Turn cakes onto racks and allow to finish cooling. Frost. *Serves 10-12.*

To prepare icing: In a large bowl, cream butter and cream cheese. Beat in sugar. Blend in vanilla and nuts. If too thick, thin with a little milk. Beat until creamy.

A layer cake is done when it shrinks away from the sides of the pan slightly and springs back from a light touch.

CHOCOLATE SHERRY BARS

1st layer

4	ounces unsweetened baking chocolate
1	cup butter
4	eggs, beaten
2	cups sugar
1	cup flour
½	teaspoon salt
1	teaspoon vanilla

2nd layer

½	cup butter, softened
4	cups powdered sugar
¼	cup whipping cream
¼	cup sherry
1	cup pecans, chopped

3rd layer

3	ounces chocolate bits
1½	Tablespoons water
2	Tablespoons butter

To prepare 1st layer: Preheat oven to 325°. In double boiler, melt chocolate and butter. Cool. In a large bowl, gradually add sugar to eggs. Stir in chocolate mixture, flour, salt and vanilla. Beat 1 minute. Pour into greased and floured 10x14-inch glass baking dish. Bake 25 minutes. Cool.

To prepare 2nd layer: Combine all ingredients. Spread over 1st layer. Chill.

To prepare 3rd layer: In double boiler melt chocolate, water and butter. Dribble over layers. Freeze. Before serving, slice into 2-inch bars. *Makes 3 dozen.*

CHOCOLATE TRUFFLES

12	ounces milk chocolate	1½	Tablespoons Amaretto or Kahlua liqueur
4	Tablespoons unsalted butter, melted		unsweetened chocolate, grated in food processor
¾	cup whipping cream, scalded		

In food processor fitted with metal blade, finely chop milk chocolate. With processor running, pour butter and cream through feed tube and process for 1 minute. Add liqueur and process briefly. Pour into medium bowl. Chill overnight. Shape into balls and roll in unsweetened chocolate. Store in freezer until ready to serve. *Makes 4 dozen truffles.*

POACHED CHERRIES

2	cups water	1	vanilla bean
1	cup sugar or to taste	1½	pounds fresh, tart cherries, pitted
	juice of 1 lemon		
	zest of 1 lemon		

In a large saucepan, combine sugar and water. Add juice, zest and vanilla bean. Bring to a boil. Boil 2 minutes. Stir in cherries. Lower heat and cook gently until cherries are slightly soft, 5-7 minutes. Do not overcook. Strain and transfer cherries to a serving bowl. Boil remaining syrup until fairly thick and reduced to 1 -1½ cups. Remove from heat and cool slightly. Remove vanilla bean. Pour syrup over cherries. Serve cool or chilled over vanilla ice cream. *Makes 2 cups.*

STRAWBERRY TUNNEL CREAM CAKE

1	10-inch angel food cake	2	cups sliced fresh
1	8-ounce package cream		strawberries
	cheese, softened	3-4	cups sweetened
1	14-ounce can sweetened		whipped cream
	condensed milk		additional fresh
1/3	cup fresh lemon juice		strawberries (optional)
1	teaspoon almond		
	extract		

To make the tunnel in the cake, cut entire top from cake one inch down using a sharp knife. Set aside. Then cut out center of cake, leaving a 1-inch wall on the outside center and bottom of cake. Reserve cake pieces. In a large bowl, beat cheese until smooth. Stir in milk, lemon juice and extract until well blended. Fold in reserved cake pieces and fruit. Spoon mixture into tunnel of cake. Replace with top of cake. Chill 3 hours or until set. To serve, garnish with whipped cream and additional strawberries. *Serves 12.*

ORANGE BLOSSOM

1	scoop vanilla ice cream	1	jigger gin
1/2	scoop orange sherbert		

Place all ingredients in a blender and blend until smooth.
Serves 1.

Note: This is easily tripled or quadrupled for more servings.

PUMPKIN SUPREME

40	ginger snaps, crushed	1/4	teaspoon nutmeg
1	cup canned pumpkin	1/2	cup chopped pecans
1/2	cup sugar	1	quart vanilla ice
1/2	teaspoon salt		cream, softened
1/2	teaspoon ginger		whipped cream
1/2	teaspoon cinnamon		additional chopped pecans

Cover the bottom of a greased 9-inch square pan with 1/2 of ginger snaps. Set aside. In a large bowl, combine pumpkin, sugar, salt, spices and nuts. Fold in ice cream. Spread 1/2 of pumpkin mixture over crumbs. Top with remaining crumbs, then pumpkin. Freeze. To serve, remove from freezer. Cover with whipped cream and nuts. *Serves 12-14.*

Make vanilla sugar by storing two vanilla beans in a tightly closed container of granulated sugar. Vanilla sugar is wonderful to sweeten whipped cream and in making dessert drinks.

ESPRESSO ICE CREAM PIE WITH CARAMEL AND RASPBERRIES

Pie

1   9-inch chocolate cookie crumb crust, prepared
1   quart vanilla ice cream
4   Tablespoons instant espresso coffee
½   pint fresh raspberries or 1 pint fresh strawberries

Caramel Sauce

1   cup sugar
1   cup water
1   cup whipping cream
⅛   teaspoon salt
1   teaspoon vanilla extract

To prepare pie: Freeze prepared crust. In a food processor fitted with the metal blade, process ice cream and coffee until smooth, using the pulse switch. Spoon into frozen crust. Freeze. Ten minutes before serving, remove pie from freezer. Pour chilled sauce to cover the bottom of 6-8 individual plates. Slice pie into 6-8 pieces and place each piece over sauce. Garnish with fruit and serve immediately. *Serves 6-8.*

To prepare sauce: In a large, heavy saucepan, combine sugar and water. Cook over medium heat, without stirring, 10-15 minutes or until sugar turns a light golden brown. Remove from heat and stir in cream until smooth. If sauce becomes hard, return to heat briefly. Allow sauce to cool 30 minutes at room temperature. Stir in salt and vanilla. Transfer to a blender and blend until ultra-smooth. Chill.

In 1904 the ice cream cone made its debut on the American scene.

KAHLUA BARS

8   Tablespoons butter, softened
1   pound dark brown sugar
2   eggs
1¼ cups flour
2   teaspoons baking powder
1   teaspoon salt
3   Tablespoons Kahlua
1   teaspoon vanilla
1   cup chopped pecans or walnuts

Preheat oven to 350°. Butter a 11¼ x 7½ x 1½ inch pan. In a large bowl, cream butter and sugar until fluffy. Beat in eggs. Add flour, baking powder, salt, Kahlua, vanilla and nuts and stir just until blended. Batter will be stiff. Pour into prepared pan and bake for 30 minutes or until tester inserted in the middle comes out clean. Cool on rack before slicing into bars. Freezes well. *Serves 16.*

Note: For an elegant presentation, bake in 2, 9-inch pie pans. To serve, place slice over raspberry sauce. Top with vanilla ice cream and chocolate sauce flavored with Kahlua.

JAMAICA SAUCE

½   cup brown sugar, firmly packed
1   ounce dark rum
1½ ounces Grand Marnier
2   cups sour cream
    fresh fruit

In a medium bowl, combine brown sugar, rum and Grand Marnier. Whisk until sugar dissolves. Add sour cream and whisk until liqueur is fully incorporated. Serve as dip for fresh fruit. *Makes 2½ cups.*

PRALINE CUPS

3	Tablespoons butter, melted	1/4	cup finely chopped pecans
1/4	cup lightly packed brown sugar	1/3	cup flour
2	Tablespoons light corn syrup	1/8	teaspoon salt
			vanilla, pecan or praline ice cream

Preheat oven to 350°. In a medium bowl, combine all ingredients except ice cream until well blended. Place 1 rounded Tablespoon of dough on a large, greased cookie sheet 3 inches from the top. Spoon another Tablespoon 3 inches from the bottom, making 2 cookies per sheet. Flatten dough with spoon and bake until cookies start to brown lightly, 6-8 minutes. Remove from oven and immediately reshape any uneven cookies into circles with the edge of a spatula. Cool 2-3 minutes. Remove cookies from sheet and invert over lightly greased, upside-down custard cups. Cookies will harden immediately. To serve, gently remove cookies from cups and fill with ice cream. Serve immediately. *Makes 4-5 cookie cups.*

RAISIN PECAN BREAD PUDDING WITH BOURBON SAUCE

Pudding

1	stale loaf French bread	1/2	cup chopped pecans
1	quart milk	1	cup raisins
3	eggs, beaten	1	Tablespoon butter, melted
2	cups sugar		
3	Tablespoons vanilla		

Bourbon Sauce

1/2	cup butter	3	Tablespoons bourbon whiskey
1	cup sugar		
1	egg		

To prepare pudding: Preheat oven to 350°. Tear bread into large pieces and place in a large bowl. Add milk and let soak until bread is soft. Add remaining ingredients except butter and blend well. Pour butter to coat the bottom of a heavy 7x11-inch oblong cake pan. Pour batter over butter. Bake 1½ hours or until very firm. Serve warm, sliced into squares with sauce poured over each piece. *Serves 8-10.*

To prepare sauce: In a medium bowl, cream butter with sugar. Transfer mixture to the top of a double boiler and cook until very hot and sugar has dissolved. Transfer to a blender or food processor. With machine running at top speed, add egg. Cool slightly. Just before serving, stir in bourbon.

When a recipe says "coats a spoon" a good test is to run your finger through the mixture on the back of the spoon. If the mixture does not run back together (leaves a stripe on the spoon) the custard is ready.

CRÈME CAMEMBERT

8	ounces cream cheese, softened	2	Tablespoons lemon juice, or to taste
4	ounces Camembert cheese(rind removed) or bleu cheese	½	cup powdered sugar
3	Tablespoons mayonnaise	8	Tablespoons unsalted butter, softened

In an electric mixer or food processor fitted with a metal blade, beat all ingredients, adding more lemon juice if desired. Pour into serving bowl or line 2½ cup decorative mold with plastic wrap. Fill with mixture, pressing to fill mold. Chill for several hours. Unmold and gently remove plastic wrap. Serve with fresh fruit.

CUSTARDS GRAND MARNIER

1½	cups milk	⅓	cup sugar
1½	cups whipping cream	¼	cup Grand Marnier
3	large whole eggs		fresh raspberries or
3	large egg yolks		strawberries

Preheat oven to 375°. In a medium saucepan, scald milk and cream. In a large bowl, whisk eggs, yolks and sugar. Add milk mixture in a steady stream, whisking constantly. Stir in liqueur. Pour into 8 one-half cup ramekins. Set ramekins in a baking dish with enough water to reach halfway up the sides. Cover loosely with foil and bake 40 minutes or until set. Remove ramekins from the water; cool. Chill at least 2 hours or up to 24. To serve, garnish with berries. *Serves 8.*

FRESH FRUIT TRIFLE

12-24	stale macaroons	2	Tablespoons sugar
½-¾	cup medium-sweet sherry	1	cup whipping cream
6	egg yolks	2	Tablespoons powdered sugar
1	cup sugar	½	teaspoon vanilla
1	pint strawberries, sliced		additional strawberries

Quickly dip macaroons in sherry and line a serving platter with them, leaving a 2-inch border on all sides. Set aside, reserve sherry. In the top of a double boiler, beat egg yolks until light. Gradually add 1 cup sugar and reserved sherry. Place over simmering water and whisk constantly until mixture coats a spoon, about 15 to 20 minutes. Cool slightly, pour over macaroons and chill. Sweeten strawberries with 2 Tablespoons sugar and spoon over custard. No more than 2 hours before serving, beat whipping cream in a small bowl until stiff. Flavor with powdered sugar and vanilla and spread over strawberries. Return to refrigerator. To serve, garnish with whole strawberries. *Serves 8.*

For best results whipping cream, chill bowl and cream before whipping.

CONTRIBUTORS

Recipes

Addington, Suegene Thomas
Adkinsson, Jan McDaniel
Albritton, Catherine Gibbs
Alsabrook, Sissy Carter
Anthony, Cindi Shannon
Ball, Charlotte Layl
Barry, Kay Arceneaux
Bell, Priscilla Rettger
Bishop, Kathy Schroder
Blanshard, Mary Cook
Bookhout, Melissa Josey
Boone, Marla Hays
Bramblett, Pedie Oliver
Bradley, Joanie Baggett
Burke, Johnetta Alexander
Byrd, Nancy Vance
Campbell, Pamela Dealey
Campbell, Susan Touchstone
Carpenter, Cele Briscoe
Clinton, Kathryn
Cochran, Julie Frost
Coerver, Holly Hunt
Coke, Anne Schoellkopf
Compton, Kelly Hoglund
Conklin, Gerre Smith
Connell, Laurie Wilkin
Cooke, Carol
Corbett, Margaret Chace
Crank, Grace Anne
Cullum, Sally Grayson
Darden, Margaret Furr
Day, Harriet Boedeker
Denton, Mary Ann Arthur
Devero, Natalie Udouj
Dillard, Susan Richardson
Dunklin, Elsie Norman
Eleazer, Joan Laprelle
Elliott, Linda Richardson
Evans, Prilly Hurley
Exall, Marion Pruett

Ferguson, Sherry Eyer
Field, Pamela Lorette
Fitch, Jane Hays
Flowers, Ellen Hunt
Fowler, Susan Downing
French, David
Gardner, Lynn G.
Geeslin, Logan Tripson
Gibbs, Harriett Weidman
Gilchrist, Jennie Malouf
Good, Becky Frost
Grace, Beth Meadows
Grant, Beverly Barley
Grant, Jane Presley
Greene, Jane Kennedy
Greer, Anne Lindsay
Haines, Cumalee Nunn
Halley, Julie
Hanks, Beth Arceneaux
Harman, Elaine McKay
Harris, Sally
Hawn, Sarah Dobson
Hewett, Petie Barry
Higginbotham, Adrienne Gaynor
Hoffman, Ellen Rodgers
Holland, Beth Ashcroft
Holman, B. R.
Horn, Priscilla Nicol
Hortenstine, Donna Wyatt
Hortenstine, Sherry Poindexter
Huddleston, Mary Hunt
Hughes, Anne Finks
Jaeggli, Caryl Nelson
Jaudes, Pamela Gridley
Jennings, Lynn Bridwell
Jordan, Biddie Banks
Kidd, Sandra Waldrep
Kilgo, Susanna Linum
Kincaid, Barbara Williams
Koontz, Ann Rogge
Kroener, Jo Anne Bergbauer
Kuzio, Janet Ray

Lambert, Paula Stephens
Lemmon, Nancy Overton
Lindsey, Jean Bethea
Longino, Gwen Mottek
Lyle, Katherine Glaze
Maberry, Kay Gibbs
Manske, Jalene Gibson
Mark, Shelby Fuqua
Marks, Sally Bateman
Marsh, Barbara J.
Marshall, Markay Hughes
Mauldin, Francis Maurice
Mauldin, Pamela "Sam" Whitelock
May, Ruth Andersson
McCall, Judy Tate
McLochlin, Nancy Dollarhide
Melson, Leslie Long
Melton, Melinda
Meyer, Peggy Manning
Mitchell, Shannon Greene
Monning, Anne Mewhinney
Montjoy, Louise
Moore, Dana Crigger
Nelson, Cathy Anderson
Norris, Debbie Conner
Norsworthy, Frances Flaig
Owen, Debbie Deering
Pace, Gail Jowitt
Pace, Margaret Streckmann
Peeler, Kittye Cowan
Priddy, Diane Young
Roberds, Susan Scheumack
Robuck, Linda Harbin
Rogers, Lucie Mahony
Rutledge, Benton
Ryan, Betsy Grant
Sands, Marcy Wilson
Saxon, Wylodean Cornelison
Sheshunoff, Jessie Cunningham
Slaughter, Linda Danielson
Smith, Janet Kerr

Smith, Joan Frensley
Sosnowski, Doris Davis
Spencer, Dody Burgher
Steele, Margaret Golden
Sullivan, Laura Edris
Teague, Byrd Fuertes
Thomas, Deborah Gullette
Thomas, Susan Turner
Trowbridge, Judith Tietze
Twombly, Meg Boggess
Utkov, Carol Carter
Vanderlind, Sarah Ford
Vineyard, Lindy Elmore
Vorhies, Linda Schoeneman
Wallace, Ann Donnohue
Wigley, Dale Cochran
Williams, Mary Roberts
Williamson, Marsha Hobin
Wilson, Elenora Kelly
Wingo, Eleesa Almand
Wittenbraker, Carolyn Kemp
Wolf, Peggy Thompson
Wood, Sally Muir
Wynn, Melinda Fly

Recipe Section Chairmen

Ball, Charlotte
Barry, Kay
Enlow, Nancy
Fitch, Jane
Gibbs, Harriet
Jenkins, Carol
Longino, Gwen
McCallum, Pam
Utkov, Carol
White, Janey

Computer Consultants

Effie and Tom McCullough

INDEX

METRIC CHART

Comparison to Metric Measure

When You Know	Symbol	Multiply By	To Find	Symbol
teaspoons	tsp.	5.0	milliliters	ml
tablespooons	tbsp.	15.0	milliliters	ml
fluid ounces	fl. oz.	30.0	milliliters	ml
cups	c	0.24	liters	l
pints	pt.	0.47	liters	l

When You Know	Symbol	Multiply By	To Find	Symbol
quarts	qt.	0.95	liters	l
ounces	oz.	28.0	grams	g
pounds	lb.	0.45	kilograms	kg
Fahrenheit	F	5/9 (after subtracting 32)	Celsius	C

Liquid Measure to Liters

¼ cup	= 0.06 liters	
½ cup	= 0.12 liters	
¾ cup	= 0.18 liters	
1 cup	= 0.24 liters	
1-¼ cups	= 0.3 liters	
1-½ cups	= 0.36 liters	
2 cups	= 0.48 liters	
2-½ cups	= 0.6 liters	
3 cups	= 0.72 liters	
3-½ cups	= 0.84 liters	
4 cups	= 0.96 liters	
4-½ cups	= 0.08 liters	
5 cups	= 1.2 liters	
5-½ cups	= 1.32 liters	

Liquid Measure to Milliliters

¼ teaspoon	= 1.25 milliliters
½ teaspoon	= 2.5 milliliters
¾ teaspoon	= 3.75 milliliters
1 teaspoon	= 5.0 milliliters
1-¼ teaspoons	= 6.25 milliliters
1-½ teaspoons	= 7.5 milliliters
1-¾ teaspoons	= 8.75 milliliters
2 teaspoons	= 10.0 milliliters
1 tablespoon	= 15.0 milliliters
2 tablespoons	= 30.0 milliliters

Fahrenheit to Celsius

F	C
200-205	95
220-225	105
245-250	120
275	135
300-305	150
325-330	165
345-350	175
370-375	190
400-405	205
425-430	220
445-450	230
470-475	245
500	260

NOTES

NOTES

NOTES

NOTES

NOTES